The Troubles

Ulick O'Connor is a biographer, playwright and poet. His biography of Oliver St John Gogarty was described by Sir Charles Petrie as 'the work of a modern Boswell' and his biography of Brendan Behan also received high praise. His book *Celtic Dawn: A Portrait of the Irish Literary Renaissance*, was described by *Newsweek* as 'remarkable, witty and fascinating.'

As a playwright he has had much success with verse plays written in the Noh form, accompanied by music and dance, which have been performed at the Dublin International Theatre Festival and off Broadway.

More recently in 1985 his play *Execution* broke the attendance record at the Abbey second theatre for a new play and his play on Oscar Wilde and Edward Carson *A Trinity of Two*, which was also performed at the Abbey, is having its French-language première in France next year.

He has performed his one-man show on Brendan Behan in Britain, Europe and the United States. He has had three books of verse published.

Ulick O'Connor was called to the Irish Bar in 1951 and practised as a barrister for fifteen years. He has been a member of the Abbey Board of Directors and is at present a shareholder of that Company.

ULICK O'CONNOR

The Troubles

The Struggle for Irish Freedom 1912–1922

Mandarin

A Mandarin Paperback

THE TROUBLES

First published in Great Britain 1975
by Hamish Hamilton Ltd as *A Terrible Beauty Is Born*
This edition revised and with a new epilogue published 1989
by Mandarin Paperbacks
Michelin House, 81 Fulham Road, London SW3 6RB

Mandarin is an imprint of the Octopus Publishing Group

A CIP catalogue record for this title
is available from the British Library

ISBN 0 7493 0177 5

Phototypeset by Input Typesetting Ltd, London
Printed in Great Britain
by Cox & Wyman Ltd, Reading

Acknowledgements

I should like to thank Bord na Mona for their help in the preparation of this edition. Eric Lasher in New York first suggested the idea. Gene Rachlis gave me much help in the development of it.

Mr Casey of the Dublin Public Libraries was especially generous in helping me to locate books. The National Library of Ireland has for many years afforded me skilful and courteous assistance. I am most grateful to them.

To Muriel Bowden, Ita Kinsella, Rita Lorigan and Pat Nolan I am grateful for meticulous work on the manuscript.

Dr Kevin Nowlan read the manuscript with his usual generosity. I thank him. The late Monk Gibbon also made invaluable suggestions.

I would also like to thank Donald Barrington, S. C.; Tom Barry; the late Colonel Eamonn Broy; Ernest Blythe; Austin Clarke; Niall Connolly; the late W. T. Cosgrave; Major-General M. J. Costello; Joe Dolan; John Dowling; the late Professor Ambrose Farrelly; Colonel Mat Feehan; Eileen Fitt; Dr Patrick Henchy; Eileen Hickey; Irish State Paper Office; Sean Kavanagh; Dr John Kelly, Leeds University; Kilmainham Jail Committee; Martin Lavan, Restoration Committee, Brighton, Michigan, U.S.A.; the late Dr Patrick Macartan; Sean McBride, S. C.; the late General Richard Mulcahy; John O'Brien; the O'Donovan Family, Rathgar; Albert Rutherford; Dr Oliver Snoddy; Seamus Sorahan, S. C.; Bill Stapleton; Major-General Joe Sweeney; Senator Trevor West; David Fitzgerald, La Touche hotel.

The quotations from the poems by W. B. Yeats, taken from *The Collected Poems of W. B. Yeats*, are reproduced by kind permission of M. B. Yeats, Miss Anne Yeats and the Macmillan Company of London and Basingstoke; the two letters written by W. B. Yeats are reproduced by permission of M. B. Yeats and Miss Anne Yeats; the poem *Remembrance* by James Stephens is reproduced by kind permission of Mrs Iris Wise and the Macmillan Company of London and Basingstoke; extracts from Sean O'Casey's autobiography are quoted by kind permission of the Macmillan Company of London and Basingstoke; extracts from two poems by A. E. are quoted by kind permission of the Estate of the late A. E.; the extract from *Seventy Years Young* by Elizabeth Fingall is quoted by kind permission of William Collins Sons & Co. Ltd.; the extract from *A Penny in the Clouds* by Austin Clarke is quoted by kind permission of Routledge & Kegan Paul Ltd.; the extract from *The History of Ireland under the Union* by P. S. O'Hegarty is quoted by kind permission of Methuen & Co. Ltd.; the quote from *The Old Woman Remembers* by Lady Gregory is reproduced by kind permission of Colin Smythe Ltd., publishers of the Coole edition of Lady Gregory's works; the extract from *Whitehall Diary: Vol. III – Ireland 1918–25* by Thomas Jones, edited by Keith Middlemass, is reproduced by kind permission of Oxford University Press. The extract from Tom Barry's *Guerilla Days in Ireland* is reproduced by kind permission of Kerryman Publications, Tralee. The photograph of Roger Casement in the German submarine is reproduced by kind permission of Dan Nolan.

Illustrations

Illustrations 1b, 6a, 11b, 14a, 23a, 23b and 24 were reproduced by kind permission of the Hulton-Deutsch Picture Library; 2, 3a, 12, 14b, 17 by kind permission of the National Museum of Ireland; 7, 8, 9, 11a, 20, 21 by kind permission of the Kilmainham Jail Historical Museum; 1a, 13b, 15a by kind permission of Picture Research-Ireland; 3b, 10 by kind permission of F. Czira; 5 by kind permission of the Irish Transport and General Workers' Union; 15b by kind permission of Michael Collins Powell; 16 by kind permission of Joe Derham; 4, 19 by kind permission of John Cashman.

Prologue

As a boy I could never understand why my father, a courteous man, could be abrupt with policemen. When confronted by the Garda Siochana he became terse. His voice snapped. If he had been driving his car, and they wished him goodbye he just grunted. He often observed that if you noticed something peculiar in a man's eye, if he wouldn't look straight at you, it would nearly always turn out he was the son of a policeman. Boys sense quickly incongruities of this sort, and I remained puzzled about it for a long time. One day my aunt gave me a hint of what might have been the cause of it. She talked to me of her grandfather, who had been Member of Parliament for East Galway, and of the policemen who stood each morning at the gate of his small estate in the West of Ireland. As he left to go into town, the policemen would take their loaded carbines down off their knees, get up on their dog cart and follow my great-grandfather into town. The reason was that, though he was then a Member of the British Parliament, he had been a revolutionary and had fought in both the Risings of 1848 and 1867. He had been one of the three members of the Supreme Council of the Fenians, the revolutionary group which organized the '67 Rising. For these reasons for the rest of his life he would be subjected to supervision by the British Secret Service. When he went to the United States, detectives followed him on board the liner at Cobh. They stayed with him throughout the voyage and opened his mail at his hotel in New York. Later when he went to Stockholm or Paris they followed him and sent back their weekly reports.

Some time ago, I went to the State Papers Office in Dublin Castle and asked to see the file on my great-grandfather. His name was Matthew Harris and he had been well known in Dublin Castle, the centre of the British administration in Ireland. When the British moved out of the southern part of Ireland in 1922 many of their secret service files were taken over by the new Government.

When the helpful young girl in charge of the library started to bring in the files connected with my great-grandfather, it became clear that the amount of material was very large indeed.

I doubt if the Tzar's Secret Police were more thorough than their British equivalent had been in Ireland. Lenin could scarcely have merited a more extensive file than my great-grandfather had.

There were photographs of him, slightly yellowed with age, looking somewhat Gladstonian. These had the name of a fashionable photographer, Lawrence, at the bottom of the photograph and had obviously been obtained surreptitiously from that source by Castle watchdogs. In the tiny meticulous handwriting of paid spies was his clandestine life chronicled. In October '69 it seemed he had received a cache of arms from Birmingham. The same month he swore in one John Murray to the Fenian Brotherhood. Matt Harris has a gun licence, one learns, and he 'roams his land at large, shooting game'. Shorthand notetakers followed him over the countryside to take down his speeches. If it became necessary to try him for some alleged conspiracy these speeches presumably would have been used against him. They are interesting to read, denunciations of landlordism, advising the people to combine because in organization lay their strength, reminding them that democracy had been achieved in America and France, and was at hand in Ireland.

That Matt Harris' eloquence and personality had gripped the West in his lifetime I knew, because his name had passed into tradition, so that as I grew up I heard him talked about with reverence, though he died before the century began.

Liam O'Flaherty, the novelist, remembers his father telling them about Harris' savage rodomontades, recalling over the breakfast table passages from his speeches that had been passed around among the people as popular ballads have been remembered elsewhere.

'Harris' words rang like the blow of a hammer on an anvil and made sparks fly which lit the country', a Mayo shepherd told a visitor forty years after Harris' death.[1]

---

[1] Told to the author by General Michael J. Costello.

Men even fought over details of his height. By West of Ireland terms of reference, a hero must be tall.

In the files in front of me I read an account of an address at Clonmacnoise, September 15, 1880, which gives us a glimpse of the old rebel's style. Clonmacnoise is a graveyard of the Irish Kings. Talking to a crowd which would have contained many frieze-coated peasants, Harris said:

Never on any former occasion when about to address a public meeting have I felt so depressed as I feel at present when I look around and see the crumbling monuments of our ancient piety and learning and heroism. Had it not been for the requirements of a public meeting, I feel that silence itself in this sacred place would be more eloquent than words.

Throughout the world, nowhere has there been found a surface of land which contains the ashes of so many saints, so many kings, and so many heroes as this locality of Clonmacnoise. Along the Causeway upon the ground on which we stand, numberless Kings have been brought here to be interred in that graveyard, and the loud re-echoing of a thousand melancholy voices has been heard hundreds of times through these valleys. Those times are all past now ladies and gentlemen; and so has the clan system vanished; the political system which existed in those times.

In this graveyard the dust of Kings has mingled with the dust of beggars and the dust of the humblest people. Not long ago in the small town of Shannon Bridge the lineal descendant of the great Maelseachlain died, a labouring man's wife. These memories, the recollection of these things I must confess sadden me. But while I feel depressed on one hand, I rejoice on the other, for the blood of these Kings circulates throughout our people. And what is the kingly power which they formerly possessed has come to be possessed by the people themselves. And if you but use that power, if you but remember that throughout the world the power of the people has pulled up Kings and Emperors and torn them down: If you can remember these things and reflect upon the might and power that rests in your own hands, you will very soon come to realize that the tearing down of Landlordism in Ireland is not such a monstrous thing as formerly you thought it was.

Many of the speeches are concerned with problems peculiar to Ireland but it is interesting to see the strain of international republicanism running through the addresses. Even then, a national agitator had to deny the charge that he was a Communist, simply because he fought for the rights of the down-trodden. Harris talks frequently of the break-up of Empire, of freedom for India, Egypt, the extension of the first challenge that had been thrown down by the United States, 'that great democracy where many of our people helped to break the chains of oppression.'

There is a change in the trend of his speeches between 1879 and 1880. Before this he is critical of those who represented Ireland in the British Parliament but by 1880 it is clear that he will go to Parliament on certain conditions.

What had happened was that he had fallen under the spell of the greatest leader Ireland had produced in the century, Parnell. Under his influence, Harris was persuaded to stand for the East Galway seat in the Summer of 1880 and was elected to the House of Commons as a Member of Parliament in that year.

There is no doubt that Parnell, by securing my great-grandfather's support, had helped to swing the Fenian Revolutionary movement behind the Parliamentary Party. Parnell's aim had been to unite the three elements in Irish life at the time, the physical force movement, the Land League and the Parliamentary Party. If he could achieve this the Irish Parliamentary Party at Westminster would hold the balance of power between the two main parties there. Harris embodied both the Fenian and the Land League traditions. Besides his revolutionary connections he had created the Tenants' Defence Association of Ballinasloe, which was the first organization to withhold rents from landlords. This method was subsequently adopted by Michael Davitt when he founded the Land League.

As I looked at the mass of papers in front of me, many of them inscribed in immaculate long-hand by meticulous civil servants, I thought of the not inconsiderable bureaucratic energy that had gone into recording the movements and utterances of one man. The lifetimes of a number of persons had been occupied with

11

the task. This is what the colonial system meant. More important even than the welfare of those governed was the task of ensuring that those who opposed the system should be silenced.

Since the end of the sixteenth century the whole of Ireland had been a dependant of England. In 1601 Hugh O'Neill, Earl of Tyrone, and his cousin Hugh O'Donnell, Earl of Tirconail, made their last stand against the Elizabethan armies at Kinsale. The Irish army was defeated and the leaders went into exile. From this time on, the administration of Ireland was in the hands of English Civil Servants who were sent to Dublin to rule the conquered nation.

In my great-grandfather's time, Ireland was governed by two men, the Lord Lieutenant (who was the King's representative) and a Chief Secretary, who was a member of the British Cabinet. Under their control was an administrative structure which included a permanent Under-Secretary, a Lord Chancellor and an Attorney-General. That this Tribune had failed to govern the country effectively was a matter of international notoriety. My great-grandfather's life span alone encompassed enough national disasters to condemn ten centuries of rule in any other country. His own father had been hanged in the rebellion of 1798 at Pallas, Co. Kildare. He lived through the potato famine of 1845–1848 which had resulted in the death of possibly a million people and the dispersal to other countries of two million more. He had taken part in the desperate stand made by the Protestant aristocrat Smith O'Brien in 1848. After that rebellion had failed Harris had gone round among the people of the West persuading them that for a while rebellion was futile and that agrarian outrages should cease.

In the four years following the famine, fifty-eight thousand families, representing three hundred and sixteen thousand people, had been evicted from their homes. They had been unable to pay their rents because of the economic depression following the famine and avaricious landlords were demanding the land on which their cottages stood for ranches. Eviction meant what it said, that the family in the house was put out and the premises, which they had often built over a lifetime, destroyed in front of their eyes. More often than not there was no place for them to go but to die by the roadside.

The most eloquent description of the state of Ireland in the nineteenth century is contained in the speech of an English Prime Minister, W. E. Gladstone, when he introduced the first Irish Home Rule Bill to the House of Commons in 1886.

Go into the length and breadth of the world, ransack the literature of all countries, find if you can a single voice, a single book – find I would say as much as a single newspaper article unless the product of the day in which the conduct of England towards Ireland is anywhere treated except with profound and bitter condemnation. Are these the traditions by which we are exhorted to stand? No: They are a sad exception to the glory of our country. They are a broad and black spot upon the pages of its history: What we want to do is to stand by the tradition to which we are the heirs in all matters, except our relations with Ireland and to make our relations with Ireland conform to the traditions of our country.

This was the system then that my great-grandfather was engaged in opposing. Because of it, though a man of property and learning, he spent the greater part of his life under the surveillance of paid spies.

But Britain at that time had little inducement to examine the results of its mis-government in Ireland. By the late nineteenth century the Empire was at its height. One fourth of the world was under British rule.[1]

From this small wind-blown island on the outskirts of Europe, Britons had gone out to conquer and rule more nations than even the Romans had done. Power was maintained to the furthest outpost of Empire by a tradition of public service. Throughout change of Government, deposition of tyrant, replacement of rajah, the loyalty to the system and incorruptibility of the British administrator remained a constant factor. They kept themselves apart from those they governed, not necessarily from a sense of superiority, but because the system demanded it. Encocooned in

[1] 'The British Government . . . now (1918) controlled well over a quarter of the human race and over a quarter of the world's land surface. The British Empire contained 450 million souls comprising representatives of practically every race and religion in the world.' Colin Cross, *The Fall of the British Empire*, London 1968.

this lifestyle, tea on the lawn, polo, cricket and hockey, dressing for dinner in the tropics, they removed themselves from contact with native cultures. It would never have occurred to this class that imperialism was as Gandhi's biographer Louis Fischer says: 'a perpetual insult for it assumes that the outsiders had the right to rule the insiders who cannot rule themselves.'

They refused to think too energetically about the rights of the governed; ideas could shatter the concept of class. The system provided them with opportunities to anaesthetize their minds against contact with those whom they ruled.

Meanwhile the performance ended, and the amateur orchestra played the National Anthem. Conversation and billiards stopped, faces stiffened. It was the Anthem of the Army of Occupation. It reminded every member of the Club that he or she was British and in exile. It produced a little sentiment and a useful accession of willpower. The meagre tune, the curt series of demands on Jehovah, fused into a prayer unknown in England, and though they perceived neither Royalty nor Deity they did perceive something, they were strengthened to resist another day.[1]

The imperial ethic was above the individual. The Irish who felt no kinship with it claimed the right to dissent.

The demand for self-determination of small nations was to become a major issue in Europe after the First War. Later the principle would be extended to include segments of society within the nation itself. Increasingly individual groups have begun to demand their rights: Women's liberation, Black liberation, American Indian liberation, Gay liberation. Even within the structure of the family children will demand a share in decision-making.

A section of the ruling class in Britain found themselves unable to accept the novel demand of the Irish to rule themselves. In the end, unable to comply with this expression of the popular will, this class chose to defy Parliament with consequences that are still felt today. In the papers strewn before me in the Irish State Papers Office in Dublin Castle, I could see the ingredients

[1] *A Passage to India* by E. M. Forster.

14

of the scheme. Repression of the individual was the rule if he would not conform. The insanity of it all. Why should that pleasant, middle-aged gentleman looking up at me from the faded yellow photograph have accepted the edicts of a system which diminished himself and demonstrably brought his people to conditions of extreme poverty?

When my great-grandfather died in 1891, the Home Rule proposals for Ireland introduced by Gladstone had been rejected. Thirty years later, the physical force organization, which he had helped to create, had brought the British flag down in Dublin and secured the evacuation of the British administration from three-quarters of Ireland.

I grew up in a free country, which was decolonized seven years before my birth. The reflexes of colonialism linger on for a time after the rulers have departed. One such remnant was my father's dislike of policemen which I have described at the beginning of this Prologue.

Chapter One

In Morley's *Life of Gladstone* there is a description of an editor coming to sympathize with Disraeli after his defeat in the General Election of 1880. The fallen Minister listened. Then looking at his friend he uttered in deep tones a single word – Ireland.

Disraeli's dismay was Parnell's achievement. By unifying the various forces in Ireland he had made it impossible for any party to rule in Britain without consideration of the Irish question. The vote of Parnell's Party at Westminster controlled the balance of power between the Liberals and Tories. This preoccupation with Ireland, according to Gladstone, had led to 'the great destruction of, and impeding of the working of Parliament'.

No Irish leader had achieved the power over his countrymen that Charles Stewart Parnell had. He was a landlord and aristocrat who had challenged the aristocracy and defied the land owners. He was not witty or eloquent as traditional Irish leaders had been. He was cold and often disdainful. When the Irish Parliamentary Party presented him with the proceeds of a public subscription which had been raised on his behalf, he took the cheque and put it in his pocket without saying a word. After Parnell had been successful in an action against *The Times* for libel he received a standing ovation in the House of Commons. He sat down without a word, ignoring the applause. 'What would they have said if I had lost', he murmured to the Member next to him.

How was it that a landlord and an aristocrat should have been converted so easily to the cause of Irish Separatism? Was it his American mother? His uncle, Charles Stewart, had been an American admiral who fought against the British in the war of 1812. Parnell's mother brought him up to dislike snobbery and superiority. When he went to Cambridge Parnell became a rebel who objected to the conventional manners of the English. 'The English look down on other races', he told his brother John. 'We, the Irish, must never look up to them. We must despise their vices.'

Parnell put the choice before England; either give Ireland self-government through constitutional methods or face the consequences of revolt. He won the support of revolutionaries because he understood the reasons for their revolt and of the constitutionalists because he provided them with a formula by which their policies could be realized.

That he was an Irish Nationalist in a separatist sense of the word, there is not a shadow of doubt. Speaking in Cork on January 21, 1885 he made his position clear: 'No man has the right to fix the boundary to the march of a Nation. No man has the right to say to his country, "thus far shalt thou go and no further", and we have never attempted to affix the *Ne Plus Ultra* to progress of Ireland's Nationhood and we never shall.'

As a little boy I once asked my grandmother whether Parnell was a great Irishman. She looked at me with amazement. I don't think the question had ever occurred to her. She accepted him not only as the greatest Irishman who ever lived but as the greatest man in the world of his time. When he came to stay with my great-grandfather in the West of Ireland, she would always come to the gate to greet him with a bunch of roses. Then he would go into the house and in a short time was deep in consultation about political matters with her father. She treasured the table on which he wrote his speeches as if it were the relic of one of her favourite saints.

My grandmother always referred to the cause of Parnell's downfall as 'Mrs O'Shea'. I learnt from her that it was not correct to refer to 'Kitty' O'Shea. Indeed, once in an unwitting moment in an article for a newspaper years later, I did refer to 'Kitty O'Shea' and received an indignant letter from a retired barrister informing me that, as a descendant of a Parnellite I should know better and never use the hated name 'Kitty'.

I don't think the morality of Parnell's adventure in love ever bothered my grandmother. She assumed that the English were responsible and had ensnared him, and to an extent she was right. Parnell had fallen in love with Mrs Katherine O'Shea, the English wife of one of the Irish Members of Westminster and had been living with her openly since 1883. Finally, dismayed at the prospect of a Liberal victory in the 1892 election and the inevitability of Home Rule, a group of Tory politicians induced Mrs O'Shea's husband to initiate divorce proceedings. This worked. Gladstone, hitherto a devoted advocate of Home Rule, but now afraid that his support of a Party whose leader had been cited in the divorce courts would lose him the Nonconformist vote in Britain, condemned Parnell and withdrew his support from the Irish Party till they replaced their leader. When a majority of the Irish Party rejected Parnell, predictably the Irish bishops moved in for the kill.

Parnell died in Bournemouth in 1891 at his wife's house. (He had married Kitty O'Shea the previous year.) His funeral fulfilled the voluptuous appetite of the Irish for tragedy. The coffin was drawn in silence through Dublin past stricken crowds who stood in the streets in numbers that have never been equalled since. As the coffin was being lowered into the grave, a falling star lit the sky. Thousands saw it.

To an extent it is true to say that the Irish never got over Parnell's death. His achievement showed the capability of the people under leadership. His downfall brought to the surface less worthy characteristics. Twenty years after Parnell's death, James Joyce would say: 'To their eternal credit the Irish never threw Parnell to the wolves. They tore him to pieces themselves.'

Parnell's memory would haunt Irish writers for decades. Denis Ireland, a Belfast Presbyterian, writes of how fifty years after his death, 'the mention of Parnell's name is as if someone had exploded a battery of depth charges deep down among the black sea caves and sunken wrecks of the Irish mind'.

As late as 1937 in a fit of passion Yeats would sit down and write:

> Come gather round me, Parnellites,
> And praise our chosen man;
> Stand upright on your legs awhile;
> Stand upright while you can,
> For soon we lie where he is laid,
> And he is underground;
> Come fill up all those glasses
> And pass the bottle round.

And here's a cogent reason,
And I have many more,
He fought the might of England
And saved the Irish poor,
Whatever good a farmer's got
He brought it all to pass;
And here's another reason,
That Parnell loved a lass.

And here's a final reason,
He was of such a kind
Every man that sings a song
Keeps Parnell in his mind.
For Parnell was a proud man,
No prouder trod the ground,
And a proud man's a lovely man,
So pass the bottle round.

Sean O'Faolain in his novel *Bird Alone* has described the eerie calm that settled in Cork on the day of Parnell's death, as a band loyal to the Chief played through empty streets in tattered uniforms.

The famous Christmas Dinner scene in Joyce's *A Portrait of the Artist as a Young Man* is typical of the divisions that occurred in many families for decades after the Chief's death.

As a student, I used to meet P. S. O'Hegarty, Sinn Fein writer and historian, who lived near me, walking to the bus. I said to him once that he seemed to show great reverence for Parnell and Gladstone in his writing. He pursed his bushy grey moustache, looked at me over his glasses and said emphatically: 'Two ghosts brooded over my boyhood in Munster and the cottages there. One was the ghost of Gladstone, the last statesman anywhere with moral courage, and the other the ghost of the Chief, a pale, indomitable, fighting ghost.'

Chapter Two

After Parnell's death Ireland was in a state of paralysis. Politicians who had seemed large men shrank overnight. The Irish Party split into segments of small men.

But another movement had been gathering throughout the nineteenth century whose impetus was to fill the gap created by the national crisis. There was to be a major revival of interest in the culture of Gaelic Ireland. As Ireland had become largely English-speaking in the nineteenth century, Gaelic culture had gradually gone underground. Scholars studied it in manuscripts preserved in libraries. In those parts of Ireland which were still Gaelic-speaking, the old culture was still miraculously alive. But the educated classes who spoke only English had lost touch with this Gaelic tradition, described by the Cambridge scholar, Robin Flower as 'Perhaps the liveliest and most concise and the most literary in its turn of all the vernaculars of Europe.'

Then, in 1893 the grouse-shooting son of a Protestant parson from Frenchpark in Co. Roscommon decided to form an association to promote the revival of the Irish language. He had grown up surrounded by Gaelic-speaking people. After he had laboriously learnt to speak the language, he discovered that the labourers, as they swung their scythes in the fields often recited poems to each other that had the courtly quality of Provençal verse. Douglas Hyde had gone round among the people, taking down their poems and stories as he heard them and publishing them later in translation. His purpose in founding the Gaelic League was to revive the Irish language among all classes of Irishmen and bring them in touch with their ancient culture.

The success of the new organization was astonishing. By 1906 there were over 3,000 branches in Ireland. By no means all Gaelic Leaguers were Nationalists. Many were Protestant Unionists who shared the general enthusiasm for reviving the ancient tongue of the country.

The Gaelic League was to have a powerful effect in awakening the Irish national conscience. The founding of the Gaelic Athletic Association was another event which would have widespread influence. The GAA, as it became known, was founded in 1884 and its purpose was to encourage Irish games and pastimes. Hurling, an ancient game which is mentioned in the sagas of Cuchulain, the Irish epic hero, was organized on a national basis and All-Ireland competitions instituted. This was a stirring pastime out of which field hockey had evolved, though in hurling the ball is kept in the air, not on the ground. Rules for 'Gaelic Football' were drawn up, a mixture of local tradition and rugby and soccer. The success of the Gaelic Athletic Association was instant. Their sporting occasions became a meeting place for men of different parishes. A patriotic atmosphere was engendered. Above all, it drew young men away from the atmosphere of the Garrison, which separatist Ireland considered sapped the spirit of the Nation.

One of the people who had been inspired by the interest in the Irish language inaugurated by Douglas Hyde was a widowed lady with a title who lived on an estate near Gort, County Galway. Her name was Augusta Lady Gregory. She was the widow of Sir William Gregory, former Governor of Ceylon. After she had acquired a rudimentary knowledge of the language through Hyde's encouragement Lady Gregory began to go down among the people, collecting legends and poems in the cottages and workhouses. Later she translated what she had collected and published them in England. Presently her work began to attract the attention of writers who were intrigued that an aristocrat of Garrison stock should delve into native culture.

George Moore, the novelist, and Edward Martyn, the Galway landlord-playwright, were among her first converts. But it was when she drew the poet W. B. Yeats into the net of Irish folklore that the movement made a real advance. At this time Yeats was a poet of the Celtic twilight, a pre-Raphaelite, writing about the Irish past as William Morris, Ruskin and Rossetti had written about the Arthurian period. Under Lady Gregory's influence he was introduced to the heroic literature of ancient Ireland out of which he was to create the symbolic figures that would dominate his plays and bring a hardness and earthy quality to his verse. Lady Gregory, Yeats and John Millington Synge were to found the Abbey Theatre in 1904 for the purpose of presenting Irish plays.

Through the Abbey Theatre, the impetus of the Irish Ireland movement was maintained. As people saw their lives mirrored on the stage, plays poured in daily to the directors, written by doctors, lawyers, dairymaids, soldiers, schoolteachers and as in Sean O'Casey's case, labouring men. Today this period has been recognized as a Renaissance, the golden age of Irish literature. Among the writers it produced in the first two decades of the century were (besides Yeats and Joyce) Sean O'Casey, J. M. Synge, Oliver St John Gogarty, James Stephens, George Russell, George Moore, Padraic Colum, Lord Dunsany, Katherine Tynan.

An energy was unleashed in the national being which affected everyone who lived then. A new nation was being born, neither Gaelic-Irish nor Anglo-Irish, but a blend of both. Such moments in a people's history are productive of great art. What John Adington Symonds has written of the Elizabethan and Florentine renaissances can be applied to Ireland at this time: 'There is a heritage of power prepared for them at birth. The atmosphere in which they breathe is so charged with mental energy that the least stirring of their special energy brings them into contact with forces mightier than the forces of single nature.'

Yeats recognized the metamorphosis that was taking place in the national being and sought to find a principle of unity, that would 'Bind the peasant visionaries that are, the landlord duelists that were, in one Celtic phantasmagoria'.

Yeats' friend, A. E. (George Russell), spoke of the First Born of the Coming Race, a composite of Anglo-Irish and Gaelic-Irish, Catholic and Protestant.

> One river born from many streams
> rolled in one blaze of blinding light.

It was a Golden Age. All who lived at that time felt the elation in the air and were affected by it. As James Stephens, one of its poets, said: 'The mind was up. What it was up to no one knew or cared.'

Chapter Three

Let us take a look at the social life of Dublin at the turn of the century. If you were not aware of the ferment beneath the glitter, it had all the appearances of an elegant imperial city. In the parks, military bands play the airs of Empire. Tall monuments rear into the sky to commemorate the victories of British generals and admirals. There are numerous barracks throughout the city, gracefully constructed, in which daily the martial pageantry of the largest army in the world is enacted. In the Phoenix Park, on ceremonial occasions regiments of red-coated infantry men, and blue jackets hauling field guns marched past, followed at the finish by cavalry squadrons who charged by at full gallop.

One day, as the band of the Royal Hussars was playing 'God Save the King' to finish a concert in the Hollow of the Phoenix Park, a shower of bricks hurtled down; but that was something to forget about and wasn't typical of the attitude of the citizens.

From January to St Patrick's Day, the city is a centre of social life for the occupants of great houses all over Ireland. 'I have been told', writes Lady Fingall, 'that for magnificence and brilliance only the Indian Viceregal Court with its mingling colours of East and West, can compare with the Dublin Castle season.'

During the 'season' the debutantes came up to Dublin to be presented to the Viceroy, the King's representative in Ireland. The young ladies stayed in the Shelbourne Hotel in Stephen's Green or in the big Georgian mansions in Fitzwilliam or Merrion Square. Dublin had a number of Court Dressmakers who catered solely for those who attended 'Court'. At night the great Georgian windows of the houses in the squares were lit up as dances began. Waltz music floated out through the doors into the vast emptiness of the squares. In the mornings, the young girls would sleep on after their late night but in the afternoon they would be up, watching anxiously at the windows for the mounted orderlies who came riding through the streets, delivering invitations to the Castle balls and parties. The fevered anticipation surrounding this complicated system of social encounter is described in George Moore's 'A Drama in Muslin'.

The main event of the season was the Ladies Drawing-Room when the debutantes were presented to the Viceroy. The Countess of Fingall has given this account in her memoirs.

There was a crowd about the gates of the Castle. The Dublin poor always turned out to see any sight that there was. They shivered on the pavement in their thin, ragged clothing, waiting for hours sometimes, so they might see the ladies in their silks and satins and furs step from their carriages into the warmth and light and gaiety that received them. The poor were incredibly patient. Even then I was dimly aware of that appalling contrast between their lives and ours, and wondered how long they would remain patient.

We drove into the Castle Yard by the private entrance. The MacDermots, having an official position which gave us this privilege, descended from our carriage and went in with crowds of other shivering debutantes and their sponsors. I remember the alarm in which, after we had divested ourselves of our cloaks, I followed Madam MacDermot up the red-carpeted stairs into one of the crowded ante-rooms where we waited until our names were called. That waiting was agony, as bad as later hunting mornings when we waited at Meets in a frozen trance, with other frozen, speechless figures, for the signal to move off that should release us. Supposing one's hair collapsed? How could it stand the weight of the feathers and long tulle lappets? And how should one ever manage one's train? Men came and went in gay uniforms. In ten minutes perhaps it would be over, and one would be still alive. (Would one be?) And one's curtsey? Could one be sure of it? Supposing one wobbled and fell at Their Excellencies' feet! Well. One could not practise it now!

An ADC in the doorway. A name that sounded like one's own.

The Throne Room was picturesque on such an occasion. I saw it clearly later. Not then, when it swam before my frightened eyes. But there, unmistakably, was Lord Spencer with that long red beard again. In Court dress with glittering orders. But it is the beard that I remember. In those days the Lord Lieutenant kissed each of the debutantes as they were Presented – an ordeal for both. I can remember now the feeling of that long thick red beard against my cheek, tickling it. Then it is over, and now I curtsey to the lovely golden-haired, rose and white, but rather pompous-looking lady in her glittering jewels, beside Lord Spencer, and walk backwards a few steps as I have been taught to do; without, I pray, falling over my train. An ADC picks it up and replaces it on my arm, and the ceremony is over.

The social life which surrounded Dublin Castle was remote from the literary renaissance. The activities of Yeats, Synge and Lady Gregory would have been looked on as 'quaint' with a slightly rebel touch.

But not all of the ladies who attended the Lord Lieutenant's *levée* had remained faithful to the social tradition they came from. There was Miss Gonne, for instance. She was the daughter of a British officer at the Curragh and was quite startlingly beautiful. Indeed, Wickham Stead, the editor of *The Times* who had seen her at St Petersburg declared her to be 'the most beautiful woman in Europe'. Miss Gonne, however, had proved tiresome and had actually gone down to the West of Ireland and organized people against evictions there. For a while she had lived in Paris and run a one-man press agency which dealt with the misdeeds of the British in Ireland. When Queen Victoria had come to Ireland for the Jubilee celebrations in 1900, instead of welcoming her, Miss Gonne and the Socialist, James Connolly, had impertinently carried a black coffin through Dublin's main street in derision.

What could have come over her? Many of the older ladies remembered her at Castle balls, and she had been a frequent attender at Afternoons in the Viceregal Lodge. Everyone loved her company, especially the old Generals, who insisted on coming every time they knew she was there, just to sit and chat with the brilliant gel. When she galloped through the Phoenix Park in the morning, her fair hair streaming in the wind, young officers used to stroll out from barracks to gaze at her.

Later she will bewitch Yeats, but when he tells her he can't be happy without her he is told by this stern Pallas Athene: 'Oh, yes you can, because you make beautiful poetry out of what you call your unhappiness and you are happy in that.'

Then there was Constance Gore-Booth, the daughter of Sir Henry Gore-Booth of Lisadell in Sligo. They were an old titled family which had given service to the Empire for generations. Constance was very beautiful and was renowned in aristocratic circles for her fearlessness in the hunt. She was regarded as the best horsewoman in the West and in a countryside where eight barred fences were not uncommon, such recognition meant a good deal. She had been presented at Court to Queen Victoria and had seemed such a nice girl before she married the Polish Count Casimir Markievicz. The Count had introduced his wife to Bohemian circles in Dublin and she had become acquainted with Mr Yeats, A. E. and the notorious Miss Gonne.

Maud Gonne had founded an organization called 'Inghini na hEireann' (Daughters of Ireland) which Constance soon joined. This group was dedicated to the cause of Irish freedom and to obtaining equal rights for women. The ladies frequently presented tableaux vivants with large casts, depicting stirring events from Irish history: many of them, it must be admitted, unflattering to the English in Ireland. Constance Markievicz was said to have devised the more graphic ones.

All Dublin remembered the night at St Teresa's Hall in Clarendon Street at Christmas 1902 when an old, bent woman had straightened up on the stage, her rich golden hair cascading over her pale face and burning eyes and Maud Gonne had spoken Yeats' words about Ireland's patriot dead.

> They shall be remembered forever
> They shall be alive forever
> The people shall hear them forever.

The drums were throbbing in the background. But Castle society closed its ears to the native beat.

Dublin was a small city then, about 400,000 people. If you walked down Grafton Street at this time, you might see five or six well-known figures in half an hour. Perhaps Oliver St John Gogarty would saunter down, in his primrose-coloured waistcoat, arm in arm with his fellow student, James Joyce. They would whisper in each other's ear, and break into gales of laughter, engaged in what Padraic Colum called 'an apostolate of irreverence', satirizing Church and State in limericks and bawdy poems. Gogarty is already recognized as a poet and Joyce is working on his first book of verse *Chamber Music*. Later he will join Gogarty out at the tower which his friend has rented and begin the work on his novel.

In St Stephen's Green you might see a middle-aged man with porcelain-blue eyes and a pink face strolling amongst the gardens. If you know Manet's famous portrait it is easy to recognize him. It is George Moore, leading novelist in the English language of his time, come back to Dublin because he sensed that a renaissance was in progress. He says he is disgusted with London. The English language is become 'A dry shank bone in the dust heap of Empire'. He has visions of argosies sailing up the Liffey and poets singing in the bowers of Merrion Square. Naturally petulant, he has just (shortly after his arrival) announced his renunciation of Catholicism and written to the papers to say that he has joined the Protestant Church. The reason he has given to the papers is the one likely to cause the most scandal. 'The Priests are wearing the King's racing colours on their vestments.' His present pose is anti-British and he will write a play in French, have it translated into Gaelic by a scribe from the Gaelic League and retranslated again into English by Yeats. Then it is to be presented at the Gaiety Theatre at the expense of Edward Martyn, his fellow landlord and cousin from County Galway.

It was impossible in those days to walk through Dublin without at one time or another, encountering a serious looking man, with a huge beard, on a bicycle. This is George Russell (A. E.), mystic and poet of the occult. He is a very good poet indeed and is surprised when Yeats recommends that he should accept the offer of a job from Sir Horace Plunkett, who had founded the Irish Agricultural Society to help improve the lot of the Irish tenant farmer. Yeats believed that if Russell went down among the people it would bring him closer to the unity they were seeking. Now A. E., instead of writing poems and painting pictures, goes from town to town throughout Ireland preaching the doctrine of co-operation as a means of breaking the grip of the local businessman in agricultural commerce.

If the St Lawrence O'Toole Pipe Band were out on Sundays you would notice one of the pipers, a tall short-sighted man with an intelligent, sardonic face. He is a docker well known in Gaelic League circles, and his name is Sean O'Casey. At night he haunts debating societies and clubs. A contemporary remembers O'Casey at a debate in Drumcondra: 'Neck and throat bound in the coils of a white muffler, a Jacobin of Jacobins, as his small red-rimmed eyes stab all the beauty and sorrow of the world in bursts of anti-English rhetoric.' Later, the Labour movement will absorb O'Casey's political energies, but now, strangely enough, he is notable for his anti-socialist diatribes.

When they met him people used to wonder: was James Stephens a man dressed up as a Leprechaun or vice-versa? He is an almost dwarf poet with a crooning speaking voice which can stop conversation in a drawing-room. He is writing a book called *The Crock of Gold* which is about leprechauns and someone has suggested he won't have far to go to find material. Sometimes he quivers, this little man. Not from fear but anger. For he is very anti-British presently and the subject of England's wrongs in Ireland can excite him greatly.

There is an interesting salon life in Dublin about this time. Yeats has his evenings on Monday, George Moore on Wednesday and A. E. on Sundays. If you are so minded you can go along to Stephen MacKenna's house (the translator of Plotinus) where you will hear music and good talk but you will have to speak either Greek or Gaelic for MacKenna will not tolerate the language of the foreigner at his house. At these various gatherings you might find Bernard Shaw, D'Annunzio, Augustus John, Edmond Gosse, John Singer Sargent, among others. Word had got round that a renaissance was in full swing and many hastened to get the flavour of it.

Chapter Four

What exactly was this Home Rule that everyone talked about? Simply stated it was the claim by the Irish to the right to order their own affairs. Tom Kettle, one of the young MPs at Westminster put it this way: 'Home Rule is the art of minding your own business well. Unionism is the art of minding someone else's business badly.' With the exception of the colonial class (who resided mostly in the north-east part of the country and who profited from the results of the union with Britain), Kettle's summing up would have been accepted by the majority of Irishmen.

Ireland had been ruled from England since 1170. There had been a period of near Home Rule between 1782 and 1800, when the Irish Parliament had been given a measure of freedom. This experiment ceased, however, with the Act of Union which united Britain and Ireland in one kingdom. The fragile assembly, however, which had existed for eighteen years had shown its mettle. Perhaps too much so. Though it excluded Catholics and was comprised of Protestant gentry and professional men, a genuine patriotism had begun to show itself among some of the members of the Parliament House in College Green so that it had to be bribed into abolishing itself. The British Government sensed seeds of dissidence even among the Garrison Irish. From 1801 onwards, elected Irish representatives would attend the Imperial Parliament at Westminster. To break the union with Britain and establish Home Government had been the aim of every Irish leader throughout the nineteenth century. O'Connell and Parnell had favoured constitutional agitation as a means to this. Two armed rebellions in 1848 and 1867 had been led by groups of people who thought that revolution was the only means of achieving self-government.

Throughout the nineteenth century in Ireland there had been this constant swing between Parliamentary agitation and armed revolution. Then in the first decade of the present century a

29

journalist came to prominence with a political philosophy which proposed to rely neither on parliamentary nor on physical force methods in pursuit of self-government but on a policy of passive resistance. The journalist's name was Arthur Griffith.

Griffith was born in Dublin in 1872. He was a printer and came from a line of Dublin tradesmen. After some involvement with nationalist movements in Ireland, he emigrated to South Africa in 1897. That country was not to his liking and he returned to Ireland in 1899, determined to devote himself to nationalist policies.

In 1900 he founded with a friend of his, William Rooney, the *United Irishman*. This paper was to have a profound effect on a generation of Irishmen. Its policy was separatist but it was read by people of widely different outlook and taste. In fact, the quality of its contributors made it one of the best written journals of its time. These included W. B. Yeats, Lady Gregory, James Stephens, Padraic Colum, George Bermingham, George Moore, Seamus O'Sullivan, Katherine Tynan, Oliver Gogarty. Griffith's style attracted them. He was himself a first-class journalist and his prose gave the paper its quality.

'We intend to decry the work of no Irish party', he wrote in the first issue, 'nor to belittle the character or asperse the motives of any Irish publicist who may differ from us, but we feel certain that if the eyes of the Irish nation are continually focussed on England, they will inevitably acquire a squint. For in our own experience, we have known some good Irishmen who by too constant gazing on the Union Jack acquired a degree of colour blindness, which caused them to perceive in it an emerald green tinge. To be perfectly plain we believe that when Swift wrote to the whole people of Ireland 170 years ago, that by the laws of God of nature and of nations, they had a right to be as free a people as the people of England, he wrote common sense; notwithstanding that in these latter days we have been taught that by the law of God, of nature and of nations, we are rightfully entitled to the establishment in Dublin of a legislative assembly with an expunging angel watching over its actions from the Viceregal Lodge. We do not deprecate the institution of any such body, but we do assert that the whole duty of an Irishman is not comprised in utilizing all the forces of his nature to procure its inception.'

The reference to Swift is typical. Griffith had modelled his style on the author of *Gulliver's Travels*. He loved to wander in the evening in the neighbourhood of St Patrick's Cathedral where Swift had been Dean, collecting ballads and folklore, feeling his night worthwhile if he came across some new story about the 'Dane' in the oral tradition of the people.

What sort of man is he, this obscure journalist who, twenty years later will sit at the negotiating table with Churchill and Lloyd George as representative of the Irish nation? Let us look at him now and remember him; for though he will vanish from our pages for a while, it is his policies that in the end will loosen the key-stone of British rule in Ireland.

His physical appearance is not striking. He is small, five feet five inches and walks with a slight roll. His hair is brown with fair streaks in it. His forehead is pale and straight (a sign of leadership according to Lavater, Gogarty noted) and there is a strong jaw which gives an impression of sternness. His eyes are his most notable feature; sea blue in colour of the kind which Seamus O'Sullivan, the poet, maintained was only found among the Western Joyces, of whom James Joyce was one.

People meeting Griffith for the first time were not immediately impressed. He had a taciturn quality which tended to put people off. Churchill noting this would describe him as 'That rare phenomenon, a silent Irishman'. But after Churchill had worked with Griffith over the negotiating table for three months he would write: 'Mr Griffith is a writer who has studied deeply European History and the polity of states. A man of high integrity.' Churchill's colleague, Sir Austen Chamberlain, thought Griffith the most courageous man he had ever met. James Stephens regarded Griffith as the 'greatest journalist working in the English tongue' and Gogarty, who admittedly idolized him, thought him the equal of Parnell.

James Joyce used to meet Griffith with Gogarty out at the Martello Tower at Sandycove and once praised him to his (Joyce's) brother: 'Griffith is the first person in Ireland, as far as my knowledge of Irish affairs goes, to revive the separatist ideal on modern lines.'

Though not inclined to gregariousness in public, among his circle of friends Griffith would become a convivial Dubliner. He was the centre of a literary circle which used to meet at the Bailey Restaurant and was well known for singing ballads written by himself.

This strange, unpretentious little journalist might almost have married the greatest beauty in Ireland. Griffith was in love with Maud Gonne, though in the end she married his best friend, John McBride, a dashing soldier who had led a brigade against England in the Boer War. Griffith called Maud Gonne 'Queen' to the end of his life and once thrashed an editor who had suggested in his paper that Maud Gonne was a British spy.

In 1903 Griffith began a series of articles on the achievements of the Hungarian People's Party under Francis Deak, which had succeeded in establishing a form of home rule for Hungary within the Austrian Empire. The parallel with Ireland was not difficult to show and Griffith's articles dealt with the methods Deak had employed and recommended their application to Ireland's situation in the United Kingdom.

When these articles were published in book form as *The Resurrection of Hungary*, it sold 30,000 copies in three months. This success encouraged Griffith to found a new political party which would have as its objective the separation of Ireland from England on the lines of the policy laid down by Deak. The policy would be to make Ireland self-sufficient. She would no longer be dependent on the whim of an English Parliament for the granting of Home Rule. The Irish members there would withdraw from Westminster and set up their parliament at home. The name of the party would be Sinn Fein which means in Irish 'Ourselves Alone'.

The first meeting of Sinn Fein was held at the Rotunda Round Room in Dublin in December 1905. Griffith and John Sweetman, a County Meath Squire, both spoke from the platform and were followed by Oliver Gogarty, then a student at Trinity, who criticized his fellow students for 'going unconsciously on with the hope of a snub from some officer at a British Army mess as their only ambition in life'.

A Constitution was drawn up at the meeting which contained fifteen articles. These dealt with protection of Irish industries, control of financial matters, non-consumption of articles on which duty was paid to the British exchequer, withdrawal of support from the British Armed Forces in Ireland, the creation of a Mercantile Marine and Consular Service, among other things. The vital clause was number fourteen. 'Non-recognition of the British Parliament.'

Griffith based his refusal to recognize Parliament's right to rule Ireland on the substance of British law. His argument was that the Renunciation Act of 1782 which admitted the right of an Irish Parliament to be bound only by laws enacted by the King and Parliament of Ireland, had not been repealed.

Gladstone had declared that he knew of no fouler or blacker transaction in the history of man that the making of the Act of Union, which had been put through the Commons with ill-concealed bribery. Therefore, Griffith argued, the Act of Union was invalid and the provision of the Renunciation Act was still operative and binding under British law.

The means by which he sought to have the provisions of the Renunciation Act adverted to, and the Act of Union set aside, was the abstention from Westminster of the Irish members, and the setting up of an assembly at home, until such times as the Imperial Parliament declared itself bound by the provisions of its own laws in relation to Ireland. Griffith maintained that there was an exact parallel between the state of affairs in Ireland and that of Hungary during the struggle for independence with Austria, in the nineteenth century. It was on the success of Deak's policy of abstention from the Austrian assembly that he based his claim to have discovered a solution for the problems of Ireland. 'We must retrace our steps, and take our stand on the compact of 1782 and the Renunciation Act as Deak took his on the Pragmatic sanction and the Laws of 1848.'

Griffith maintained that if the Irish members withdrew from Westminster and set up a parliament in Dublin, this parliament would function with its own civil service, judiciary, and a local government administration, established in opposition to official government institutions.

The importance of Griffith's policy rested on two factors. Firstly it had a broad practical basis which made it applicable to the various changes of political situation which could occur in

Ireland. Sinn Fein was to win an overwhelming majority in the 1918 general election, and Griffith's policy of abstentionism would be put into operation. Parliament assembled in Dublin, courts were established and a local government administration set up, side by side with the official British ones.

When Dublin Castle would suppress the passive resistance movement in 1919, it was the physical force element which had allied itself with Sinn Fein that claimed the right to resort to arms to defend their Parliament. Without the moral force of Griffith's abstentionist administration behind it, the physical force movement could not have succeeded or received the local and international support that it did.

The second factor in Griffith's Sinn Fein policy was that it envisaged a solution which would resolve the division between the two opposing forces in Ireland, Unionist and Nationalist. Griffith had included a plan for a dual monarchy in his policy. There was to be a king of Great Britain, and a king of Ireland – again on the Hungarian model. This would have provided a satisfactory imperial link for the Unionist elements. Griffith himself was by nature and conviction a separatist, that is he believed in the complete separation of Ireland from the Empire. But he recognized the existence of another class of Irishman, who did not think as he did, and it was to absorb them into the new Ireland that he devised his policy. Pragmatism was his greatest virtue. He once said, 'I am a separatist but the Irish people are not separatists. I think they can be united under this broad policy.' He was thinking of the Unionist element. It was because he devised a policy which could bring all classes of Irishmen together under a common ideal that Griffith may rank with O'Connell and Parnell as one of the three great Irish leaders in the post-Union period.

One person whom Griffith's philosophy attracted to the movement was Constance Markievicz. One day she found a copy of Griffith's newspaper lying about a hall in which she was rehearsing amateur theatricals. She was entranced by what she read and immediately joined Sinn Fein and was soon a leading member, being elected to its Council in 1909.

Both Countess Markievicz and Maud Gonne were delighted to find that Griffith supported their aspirations for freedom for women. He gave his full support to Maud Gonne's 'Daughters of Ireland', the early suffragette group formed to secure women's rights.

Another recruit to Sinn Fein was a man whose name could be found at that time in the headlines of all the British papers, next to accounts of the Royal Family's activities and the Prime Minister's speech. He was a dashing young Consul who had made world news with his publication of a report exposing atrocities in the Belgian Congo. His name was Roger Casement. During a brief holiday back in his native Antrim, in the North of Ireland, he came in contact with Griffith's paper and immediately recognized the editor as the man most likely to make headway at that time.

Chapter Five

The novelist, Joseph Conrad, after he had met Roger Casement in the Congo, wrote to a friend, 'I can assure you that he is a limpid personality. There is a touch of the conquistador in him too; for I've seen him start off into an unspeakable wilderness swinging a crook-handled stick for all weapons, with two bull-dogs, Paddy (white) and Biddy (brindle), at his heels, and a Loanda boy carrying a bundle for all company. A few months afterwards it so happened that I saw him come out again, a little leaner, a little browner, with his stick, dogs and Loanda boy, and quietly serene as though he had been for a stroll in a park.'

For A. D. Morel, an English parliamentarian, who was to defeat Churchill in the 1922 general election and narrowly miss a Cabinet post in Ramsay MacDonald's government Casement was, 'A man with an extraordinarily handsome and arresting face, a long lean swarthy van dyke type, graven with power and with all of great gentleness. From the moment our hands gripped and our eyes met, mutual trust and confidence were bred and the feeling of isolation slipped from me like a mantle. Here was a man indeed.'

Roger Casement was not at all a typical employee of Her Majesty's Consular Service. He had a bubbling Irish temperament and overwhelming charm and could mesmerize people he had just met with his sparkling conversation.

He was brought up in Antrim in the North of Ireland, of Protestant Unionist background. But his mother had been a Catholic and this may have given him an early sympathy with Irish nationalism. As a young man he had written a poem on the subject of the death of Parnell. It was as a member of the Consular Service that he came to be in the Congo. There he encountered evidence of atrocities perpetrated by Belgian colonists on natives employed in extracting the natural wealth of the country. With the encouragement of the Foreign Office, he had gone on an investigative tour of the Congo and prepared a report

36

which, when it was published, received world-wide publicity. As a result of the report, Casement became a national hero in Britain.

After the report had been published however, in 1904, Casement became increasingly disenchanted with the bureaucracy of the Foreign Office. There is a significant sentence in a letter written at this time where he claims that the Foreign Office was not able to grasp the extent of his researches because 'I looked on the Congo with the eyes of another race, of a people hunted themselves.'

His Congo researches had shown him the extent to which government by a great power could lead to degenerate conditions. If King Leopold was an unscrupulous despot on a scale unrivalled in Britain, nevertheless, the principle of Empire was the same, whether it was exercised by German, French, Dutch, Belgian or English colonists.

Back in Antrim, recovering after the rigours of his Congo experience and at the height of his fame, Casement was captivated by Griffith's policies.

The Hungarian parallel particularly appealed to Casement because his father had been one of those who had come out to join Louis Kossuth in the revolt against the Austrian Empire. We can see in Casement's reactions to Griffith's policies the insight of the trained civil servant as well as the reaction of the incipient nationalist. Casement knew imperialism from the inside. He knew the strength of the system. Now he recognized that here was a political programme which could free Ireland from the coils of mis-government.

Inspired by his contact with Sinn Fein, Casement set out to learn the Irish language, 'the lovely, glorious tongue', as he termed it. In Antrim there were still pockets of native Irish speakers and during the summer of 1905, Casement went to *feiseanna* (Irish-speaking festivals of music, dance and poetry) which were held throughout the glens.

When his old school, Ballymena Academy, wrote asking him as a distinguished past pupil to donate some money for the school fund, Casement replied saying that he had commitments elsewhere as he had promised to subsidize a school where the Irish language was taught as a living tongue and, therefore, could not subscribe to the Alma Mater. He was sending the money instead, he told them, to a summer school in Donegal run by a young Gaelic Leaguer named Eamon de Valera.

Before he left Ireland in 1906 (for the Amazon Valley) Casement had written articles in various papers advocating Sinn Fein policies. He was at this time about to be promoted in the Consular Service and had recently been made a Commander of the Order of St Michael and John by Edward VII. Casement's conversion to Sinn Fein was an indication of the influence that Griffith's political articles had at this time. In addition, as Casement was a Protestant, as were James Stephens, Maud Gonne, Constance Markievicz, Alice Milligan and George Bermingham, it is clear that Griffith had succeeded in finding a formula which could include Irishmen of different religions and racial origins in a common political aim. 'Ireland is truly no longer the Gaelic nation of the twelfth or even the eighteenth century', he wrote in his paper. 'The Gael is gone, the Dane is gone, the Norman is gone and the Irishman is here.'

Chapter Six

Popular support for Sinn Fein fell sharply in 1910. A new development in British politics had brought the Home Rule issue to life again. Except for the support of a few intellectuals, Griffith had no backing. He had persistently maintained that England would never grant Ireland self-government through the efforts of the Irish Party at Westminster. Now it seemed he was wrong and Home Rule was on the way. Via the Irish Party.

Out of office since 1893, the Liberal Party had finally been returned to Government in Britain in 1906. At that juncture the Irish Party had only just begun to reorganize and the Liberals were not inclined to promote policies which might endanger their position with the electorate.

However, a series of social enactments between 1908 and 1910 had necessitated increased expenditure which the House of Lords would almost certainly refuse to sanction. The Prime Minister, Asquith, decided to geld this body of its powers and in 1911 the Parliament Act was passed which provided that the Lords could only veto a Bill three times; after that it became law. To get the Parliament Bill through the Commons the vote of the Irish Party was essential. United at this time under the leadership of a Parnellite, John Redmond, the Party was once more in a position to bargain for Home Rule.

If the Liberal Party had relinquished Gladstonian morality, its leader Asquith was not without a sense of British pragmatism. As Robert Kee, the British author, has put it in his book *The Green Flag*, '272 Unionists opposed by 272 Liberals in a House of Commons which also contained 42 Labour and 82 Irish Nationalists equalled Home Rule. It was as crude as that.'

In April 1912 Asquith introduced his Home Rule Bill in the Commons. It seemed now that short of armed rebellion, nothing could stop it becoming law. A huge wave of enthusiasm swept over Ireland. Redmond was hailed as a great leader who would finish the work begun by his hero Parnell. From all over the world, America, Australia, South Africa, congratulations flowed in to Redmond for his achievement. Middle-class Ireland girded itself to take over the reins of government. Young men of the newly established National University practised debate in College Societies as a preliminary to taking part in parliamentary dispute and looked to the day when they would be Cabinet Members in the first Irish Government.[1]

Redmond's contribution was that he had succeeded in uniting a party that was split by dissension. Though he was a country squire with an estate in Wicklow, and with a fondness for fishing and shooting, he had a good nationalist background and one of his ancestors had been out in the rebellion of 1798. As a young man he had shown a sympathy for imprisoned Fenians and had used his influence to get many of them released. But he had one flaw. He trusted the English implicitly on Irish matters. A. M. Sullivan, the poet, once said about Parnell: 'He never dreamed of giving the English credit for good intentions. He is always on the lookout for the cloven hoof.' Redmond, on the other hand, always believed in giving credit, not recognizing that when a great power is threatened, its reactions to a small people is more likely to be dictated by pragmatism rather than justice.

In March 1912, however, it seemed as if Redmond was on the brink of settling the dispute of centuries. He would be the man responsible for bringing the first Irish Parliament into being. In the general enthusiasm the policies of Sinn Fein seemed an anachronism. The physical force movement appeared finished.

A monster meeting was held in O'Connell Street on March 31, 1912, to welcome the Home Rule Bill. Those who took part in the meeting and spoke from different platforms in the street came from all sections of political life in Ireland. Separatists, Revolutionaries, Socialists, all welcomed the Bill as a measure which would provide an opportunity for the development of the country. It is worthwhile considering the speeches of the three

---

[1] Conditions in Ireland by 1912 had improved considerably since Gladstone's time. In particular the Local Government Act of 1898 had transferred power on a local level into the hands of the ratepayers. The Land Act of 1903 had enabled tenants to purchase the fee simple of their land at a fair price from the landlord with a Government grant.

main speakers at the meeting in O'Connell Street that day. All three welcomed the Home Rule Bill.

The first speaker, John Redmond, who spoke as leader of the Irish Party, was to hold on to his belief in the Bill to the end of his life. His speech was received with wild cheering. 'Trust the old party – and home rule next year' was the message.

The second speaker was Eoin MacNeill, professor of early Irish history at the National University, president of the Gaelic League and an Ulsterman, who was two years later to found the Irish Volunteers in an effort to combat the Ulster Protestant resistance to Home Rule.

MacNeill's welcome for the Bill was more cautious but it contained positive advice to work the new measure. 'There is no law so very bad that it would not be better for the Irish people to accept if they themselves were in charge of it. If the English people have sense they will not endeavour to keep back from Ireland as much as one inch of her rights, especially in regard to the financial question and the question of taxation. We are not asking for charity but demanding our rights.'

The third speaker, Padraic Pearse, was the headmaster of an Irish-speaking school, St Enda's. He was well known in Gaelic League circles and as a poet and playwright among the literary groups. Pearse's welcome of the Home Rule Bill has a special significance. Almost four years later to the day he was to read the Proclamation of the Irish Republic in O'Connell Street as Commandant-General of an insurgent army in rebellion against British rule.

Pearse, like MacNeill, spoke in Irish. 'We have no wish to destroy the British,' he said that day, 'we only want our freedom. We differ among ourselves on small points, but we agree that we want freedom, in some shape or other. There are two sections of us – one that would be content to remain under the British Government in our own land, another that never paid, and never will pay, homage to the King of England. I am of the latter, and everyone knows it. But I should think myself a traitor to my country if I did not answer the summons of this gathering, for it is clear to me that the Bill which we support today will be for the good of Ireland and that we shall be stronger with it than without it. Let us unite and win a good Act from the British; I think it can be done.'

An extremist reading Pearse's speech next day would have been disappointed. It had a smack of Redmondism, abandoning the traditional separatist position and accepting the authority of a British Parliament to enact laws in Ireland.

But there was little support for revolution in 1912 in Ireland, or for any policy but that of the Irish Party. Arthur Griffith's influence was at its lowest. It appeared as if he had been mistaken in his mistrust of the British. The Irish people were about to get what they wanted through the efforts of the Irish Party at Westminster, whose boycott Griffith had advocated and, as a result, support had slipped away from Sinn Fein.

There were two notes of warning sounded at the meeting that day which, viewed in the context of what was to happen, have a chilling authenticity. MacNeill said at the end of his speech, 'If the last of our rights are kept from us, so much the worse for the English people – it will be a nail in the quick for them.'

Pearse finished his speech with the warning, 'But if we are tricked this time, there is a party in Ireland, and I am one of them, that will advise the Gael to have no counsel or dealings with the Gall[1] for ever again, but to answer them henceforward with the strong hand and the sword's edge. Let the Gall understand that if we are cheated once more there will be red war in Ireland.'

[1] The English

42

Chapter Seven

While in the South there was an enthusiastic reception for the Home Rule Bill, in the north-east corner of the island there was quite a different reaction to the Government's proposal.

This area, known as Ulster (one of the four historic provinces of Ireland), particularly in the north-eastern part, was predominantly Protestant as opposed to the rest of the country where Catholics were in the majority. In the whole of Ireland, Protestants formed about one quarter of the population. But one million and a quarter of these resided in the counties of Antrim, Tyrone, Fermanagh, Armagh, Derry and Down. In the remaining counties the Protestants formed about 10 per cent of the population.

The Ulster Protestant was a special breed. The majority of them had come from Britain to Ireland in the sixteenth and seventeenth centuries. Government policy had been to settle emigrant adventurers on land taken from Catholic owners. But whereas in the rest of the country there had been a unifying of personality between settler and native so that the descendants of the original planters – men like Swift, Sheridan, Goldsmith, and George Berkeley – had become more Irish in temperament than English, no such agreeable process had taken place in north-east Ulster. There the siege mentality still persisted.

The working-class Protestant was reluctant to relinquish that most cherished of concessions, the right to look down on someone else. They remained *colons* with the deeply entrenched prejudices common to this class and had developed an outlook not dissimilar to that of the poor whites in the Southern States of America during the Civil Rights agitation. As long as Ireland remained part of Britain, the position of superiority enjoyed by the Ulster Protestant would survive. But should Ireland be ruled by a Dublin Government rather than from Westminster, the fear of the Ulster Protestant was that not only would he lose his privi-

43

leged position but that retribution would be exacted for the period during which his class had held the upper hand.[1]

In itself, this situation was one which required special handling. But not only were these understandable Protestant fears not merely ignored in Parliament; unscrupulous elements in the Conservative Party deliberately exploited them for political gain using Ulster as a pawn in the struggle between the two parties at Westminster. It was Lord Randolph Churchill who first 'Played the Orange card', and succeeded in having Gladstone's first Home Rule Bill defeated in 1886, a defeat which brought down the Liberal Government of the time.

As the final stages of the struggle in Parliament between Commons and Lords began to take shape, Ulster assumed more and more importance. It was to be the last bastion where the forces of reaction could muster, confronted now not by the uncouth alphabet of the barricades, but the ordered language of statutory enactment.

On March 12, 1912, less than two weeks after the mass Home Rule meeting in O'Connell Street, Dublin, another mass meeting was held in Belfast. At Balmoral Park, a few miles from the city centre, a hundred thousand men marched in military formation past Sir Edward Carson, K. C., Member of Parliament. Carson was a Dublin barrister with powerful influence in the Conservative Party and had been Solicitor General in Balfour's Government which had preceded Asquith's. Also on the stand with him was the new leader of the Conservative Party and future Prime

[1] Not all Irish Protestants entertained such fears. George Bernard Shaw, a Dubliner, speaking at a meeting in the Memorial Hall, London, in December 1912, said:

'I cannot describe what I feel when English Unionists are kind enough to say, "Oh, you are in danger of being persecuted by your Roman Catholic fellow countrymen. England will protect you." I would rather be burnt at the stake by Irish Catholics than protected by Englishmen. I am far more anxious about the future of the unfortunate English should they lose us. What will they do without us to think for them? The English are a remarkable race; but they have no commonsense. We never lose our commonsense. The English people say that if we got Home Rule we should cut each other's throats. Who has a better right to cut them? They are very glad to get us to cut the throats of their enemies. Why should we not have the same privilege among ourselves? What will prevent it? The natural resistance of the other Irishmen.'

44

Minister, Andrew Bonar Law, a Canadian of Ulster descent. The purpose of these thinly disguised military manoeuvres was to demonstrate the strength of resistance in Ulster to the Home Rule Bill. The men marched under a Union Jack reputed to be the largest ever made.

It was a contradictory situation. These sturdy Ulstermen were prepared to use force to defy the will of Parliament in order to remain within that Parliament. An inexplicable situation, unless one remembers that they were demonstrating for the retention of privilege which would vanish as soon as the British connection was destroyed.

It is less easy to exculpate those who stood on the platform at Balmoral that day, than their stern-faced supporters marching below in flurries of bands and waving of Union Jacks. Carson and Bonar Law were to sit in the War Cabinet and Bonar Law would become Prime Minister of England. Both men were steeped in Parliamentary tradition and well aware of the drastic consequences which could result from the conspiracies upon which they were embarking. On the platform with them that day in Balmoral Park were Lord Londonderry and Lord David Cecil. Their presence did not prevent Carson from issuing threats of a startling nature coming from a former Minister of the Crown. 'They would do all that men could do,' he said, 'to defeat a conspiracy as treacherous as had ever been formed against a great nation.'

As the Ulster resistance to Home Rule gathered momentum Bonar Law and Carson began to speak more explicitly about their intentions. 'I do not care two pence whether it is treason or not,' Carson said at Coleraine a few months after the Belfast rally. 'The Attorney General says that the doctrines and course I am taking can lead to anarchy. Does he not think I know that?' he said shortly afterwards. Speaking at Blenheim, the home of the Churchill family, the Duke of Marlborough said: 'I can imagine no length of resistance to which Ulster will not go and in which I shall not be ready to support them.'

On September 28, 1912, Carson, escorted by a mounted body-guard, went to Belfast cathedral to affix his signature to the Ulster Covenant. This pledged those who signed it to: 'Stand by one another in using all means which may be found necessary to defeat the present conspiracy to set up a Home Rule Parliament and in the event of such a Parliament being forced upon us, we further solemnly pledge ourselves to refuse to recognize its authority.' After Carson, Lord Londonderry signed: then likewise the Moderator of the Presbyterian Assembly and the Protestant Bishop of Down and Connor. That day, 20,000 people signed the Covenant.

An Ulster Provisional Government 'established to control affairs in Ulster if the Home Rule Bill passed through Parliament' was set up in autumn 1912. The military aspect of Carson's defiant philosophy began to show itself after the Provisional Government was formed. The senior Field-Marshal of the British Army, Field-Marshal Lord Roberts was asked to recommend a Commander for a para-military force to be formed to resist Home Rule. Roberts suggested Lieutenant-General Richardson, a former Indian Army General who was appointed leader of the New Volunteer Force formed in April 1913.

By June, Richardson had 50,000 men under his command. These para-military troops were pledged to resist any enactment which would lead to the enforcement of Home Rule in Ireland. Carson and Bonar Law were soon joined by other members of the Conservative Party who did not scruple to use the Ulster situation as an opportunity to show their anger at Asquith's gelding of the House of Lords. F. E. Smith acted as 'galloper' for Carson, reviewing Ulster's illegal army on horseback. Smith was the most brilliant legal mind in England of his day and was later to become Lord Chancellor. Carson's most able Lieutenant in Ulster was James Craig, son of a whiskey magnate and Member of Parliament for East Antrim. In Britain a 'British League for Ulster' was formed and a hundred and twenty Members of Parliament and a hundred Peers became members. Rich supporters in Britain sent guns to Ulster for use by the Volunteers.

The word 'treason' begins to appear more and more in the frequent denunciations of Carson that were heard at this time. In Parliament, the Home Secretary, Winston Churchill, declared that: 'Bonar Law is a public danger, seeking to terrorize the Government,' and castigated Carson 'for taking part in a treasonable campaign'.

A former Justice of Appeal in Ireland, Sir James O'Connor, has written: 'That Carson's action was treasonable is beyond question. All of those highly placed men who were engaged in the Ulster campaign were guilty of the grave offence known to British law as treason, felony, punishable with penal servitude for life. The gist of the offence is this, that no man by force or show of force compel Parliament to do or abstain from doing anything whatsoever. If it were otherwise, mob law would be substituted for the will of the people expressed through Parliament.'

O'Connor was a Law Officer of the Crown at the time the Ulster Volunteers were formed and has made it clear in his book *A History of Ireland* that at one stage warrants for Carson's arrest and the arrest of other members of the Ulster Movement were made out ready to be enforced from Dublin Castle.

Why was it that events in Ulster were allowed to continue unhindered?

One reason was that the Government hoped to play for time. By the time Home Rule would have become law, they hoped that the Ulster resistance would have died down and saner views would have prevailed in the Conservative Party. Asquith, too, may have believed that the Ulster campaign was a bluff. The evidence now seems to show that it was nothing of the kind. General Crozier, a regular Army Officer who was in control of a section of the Ulster Volunteers has stated in his book *Ireland Forever* that he would have given the order to fire on army and police on one occasion had not some fortunate incident intervened.

Chapter Eight

Within a few months of the founding of the Ulster Volunteers, a similar organization had been formed in the South, only with the contrary aim of ensuring the passage of the Home Rule Bill through Parliament, rather than resisting it. This was called the Irish Volunteers.

Its founder was Eoin MacNeill, professor of Irish history in University College, Dublin, the same man who had spoken at Redmond's meeting in 1912 to welcome the Home Rule Bill. I remember as a small boy my grandfather who was a close friend of MacNeill's taking me aside and saying to me seriously one day, 'Remember when you grow up that Eoin MacNeill was a good man.' (Later I would recognize that this was a reference to an attempt to discredit MacNeill's motives because of his efforts to stop the Rising in 1916.)

My mother would talk of how each summer she and her father, and my aunt would go with MacNeill to the Aran Islands off Galway to learn Irish. There they would be lowered from a ship into currachs, rowed to the shore and would live for two months on Inisheer in the atmosphere of an Ireland which had scarcely changed since the time of Christ. My mother's family and the MacNeills would come back with Gaelic-speaking nannies to the mainland so that the children could, in an urban existence, continue to absorb the Gaelic tradition.

This is the type of background to which the founder of the Irish Volunteers, which were to have such influence on the future relations between Britain and Ireland, belonged. His world was one of scholarship, bridge on Sunday and conversation in the genteel drawing-room atmosphere of Edwardian Dublin. How is it that such a man came to found a para-military force which, within two years, would be engaged in open warfare against British troops in Dublin?

Crisis can accelerate the effect of men's actions far beyond what they intend and in MacNeill's case an article in *An Chlai-*

dheamh Soluis (The Sword of Light), a Gaelic League weekly, led to his being installed at the head of an army which he may have had no wish to lead. His article appeared on November 1, 1913. It suggested that Sir Edward Carson had shown the way in the North by his defiance of Westminster and that the South should follow suit. Carson, MacNeill argued, had 'knocked the bottom out of Unionism'. And he gave the Ulster Volunteers the curious attribution of 'Orange Home Rulers'.

It was an ingenious interpretation of the Northern crisis and was admirably suited to the aims of certain groups who awaited an opportunity to arm and drill in the open. MacNeill was approached and asked if he would agree to inaugurate an Irish Volunteer Force which would have for its objectives the peaceful passing into law of the Home Rule Act. MacNeill agreed and a number of preliminary meetings were held. Eventually, after a meeting on Monday, 11 November, at Wynn's Hotel, Dublin, a Committee of thirty was formed which included representatives from Redmond's Parliamentary Party, as well as from separatist groups.

Roger Casement was made Secretary. He was now Sir Roger Casement, having been knighted by the King for his report of a series of atrocities in the Amazon Valley, in addition to his services in the Congo. Retired from the Consular Service because of ill health, he had returned to live in Ireland and devote himself to the Irish cause. He was to be a valuable member of the new organization, speaking from recruiting platforms for them and organizing meetings throughout the country.

The opening meeting of the Volunteers at the Rotunda Concert Hall on November 25, 1913 was an overwhelming success.

There was accommodation for eight thousand but the crowds overflowed into the nearby Parnell Square and a second meeting had to be held in another hall there. Inside the Rotunda room there were representatives of every national group in the country. Robert Davitt, son of Michael Davitt, Fenian and founder of the Land League, represented Redmond's Irish Party. Padraic Pearse was there, the headmaster of St Enda's, who had spoken at Redmond's meeting at O'Connell Street in March, 1912.

49

Pearse, who was one of the invited speakers, was by now a member of the Irish Republican Brotherhood.

A deputation of eight hundred students from the newly established National University marched from the University to attend the meeting. Men from the newly formed Transport Union arrived with hurleys on their shoulders, presumably to impress the Constabulary with the fact that any interruptions from them would be returned with interest.

The meeting was held in an atmosphere of high excitement. MacNeill in his speech pointed out that that day an advertisement had appeared in the British papers for volunteers for Ulster, and that it had been signed by Lords Beresford and Castlereagh, two landlord names that had a particularly odious significance for an Irish nationalist audience. In the face of Carson's initiative, MacNeill continued, the Government had shown a 'passive attitude which amounts to a complete and cowardly surrender'. He proposed to remedy this by the formation of an Irish Volunteer Army which would assert the rights of Irishmen. He ended with the phrase, 'They have rights who dare to maintain them.'

MacNeill was followed by eight other speakers, including Padraic Pearse, who pointed out with some force that Ireland armed would strike a better bargain with the Empire than Ireland unarmed.

The first meeting of the Volunteers was an instant success. Seven thousand recruits signed on on the opening night. By January, the Irish Volunteers numbered ten thousand and by the following September there were a hundred and eighty thousand trained men. The Volunteers were drilled mostly by ex-British soldiers. In charge of training was George Moore's brother, Colonel Maurice Moore, a professional soldier who had served in the Boer War.

Chapter Nine

This plethora of military activity in both the North and South played into the hands of the Irish Republican Brotherhood, the secret oath-bound physical force organization which had been in existence since Fenian times. After Parnell's death the centre of the movement had shifted to the United States. There it operated under the umbrella of the powerful Clann na Gael organization. Clann na Gael was run by John Devoy, an ex-Fenian and former French Foreign Legionary, who had served long sentences in British jails before being deported to the United States. He was a sturdy old rebel with a single purpose in life, the breaking of the British connection in Ireland.

In the second half of the nineteenth century the Dynamite Party (that was their actual name), operating from New York, had sent a steady stream of bombers to destroy buildings and public installations in Britain. Some were caught and sentenced to life imprisonment. Political prisoners underwent stern treatment in Britain at that time and a number of Irishmen went mad while serving their sentences. One of those who survived was Thomas Clarke. He was released on ticket of leave in 1896. He went immediately to New York where he became an important figure in Clann na Gael. Clarke was dispatched to Ireland in 1907 with orders from Devoy to reorganize the I. R. B. there. He set up a tobacconist shop in Parnell Street just off O'Connell Street which was to be used as a recruiting centre. Clarke would not have many recruits in the first few years. The spirit of the time was against the I. R. B. but those he enrolled formed an elite group.

P. S. O'Hegarty, the historian, who was himself a member of the I. R. B., has recalled how the organization recruited at this time.

From the Gaelic League, the G. A. A., the Clubs and the literary societies, the I. R. B. recruited slowly and carefully, and began to build a small but effective and formidable organization behind organizations. It did not look for numbers but it did look for quality. There was no general and no careless recruiting. Nobody who habitually drank to excess, nobody who kept bad company (i.e. frequented police or soldiers or people known to be undesirable nationally) and nobody of bad character was recruited, and no centre had the power to recruit anybody of his own volition. Before any direct approach was made to anybody, he had first to be proposed at a meeting of a circle, his sponsor there having to be fully acquainted with his character and his sentiments. If nothing was known against him at the circle, the name was circulated in the other circles of the district, and permission to recruit him was not given until any doubts expressed about his suitability were cleared up. It was rare, but it did happen sometimes, that a serious objection was raised in one of the other circles. Nobody of a low standard of intelligence was recruited.

It is not insignificant that Yeats was a member of the I. R. B. The organization looked up to intellect. Many of the leaders were well read in European literatures and the philosophy of revolution. They made frequent trips to Stockholm and Paris to discuss tactics with other groups engaged in plotting the downfall of Empires.

The I. R. B. was not without elitist tendencies. There had been several appeals by I. R. B. leaders to Anglo-Irish landlords to join them against the common enemy, England. They looked up to breeding of any kind whether it came from cottage or castle, regarding it in the Gaelic tribal sense as a principle of leadership.

Yeats' I. R. B. friend, John O'Leary, used to say 'My motto is the Persian one, to pull the bow and tell the truth,' and he would maintain that there were things a man should not do even to save a nation and one of them was to cry in public.

Tom Clarke was understandably elated after the Irish Volunteers were founded. The new organization would provide a cover for the I. R. B. Only the year before with the Home Rule Bill on everyone's lips the revolutionary movement had seemed in danger of perishing. Now by careful planning the I. R. B. had five men on the Committee of the Volunteers. These were Con Colbert, Michael Lonergan, Liam Mellows, Sean O'Connolly, and Padraic O'Riann. After some time they would control the organization.

Behind the counter of his tobacconist shop Clarke recruited steadily from now on. He was happy that the Revolution seemed in sight at last. Those fifteen terrible years in jail hadn't been in vain. One of those whom he swore into the I. R. B. was Sean O'Casey who has left us a picture of this unrepentant Fenian.

Fifteen years of distorted life in jail, added to fifteen years of silent defensive fighting for mind and body, had fretted away the outward semblance of strength and virility. The full and happier growth of his life had been sucked away into useless-ness and pain. Almost all his loyalties in the colours and enjoyments of life had been burned away, leaving but a slen-der, intense flame of hatred to what he knew to be England. Free himself, now, he plucked impatiently those who wanted to let bad enough alone. Watch him locking up his tiny shop, slipping the key in his pocket, then giving a swift turn to where a Committee waited for him; a warm, rough, tweed overcoat belted firmly at his slender waist, a broad-brimmed hat set firm on his greying head, the frail figure went straight on, taking short, rapid steps with a tiny spice of jauntiness in them; straight on, looking neither right nor left, to where a drooping Committee sprang to interested alertness when he came among them, and bent low over the task of moulding the bullets that would tear rough and roguish gaps open in some of their own breasts.

Chapter Ten

From August 1913 until Christmas of that year, Dublin was paralysed by a massive labour strike. The immediate result of the strike was to consolidate working-class resistance to the establishment. It also resulted in the creation of yet another paramilitary group, the Citizen Army, formed from men who had been involved in the strike.

The workers were led by two remarkable men, Jim Larkin and James Connolly. Connolly was later to be executed as one of the leaders of the Rebellion. Larkin who was of Irish parentage had come to Ireland from Liverpool in 1906. He became General Organizer for the National Union of Dockers in Ireland, opening a branch in Belfast and then coming to Dublin to organize it there. In 1908 he founded the Irish Transport and General Workers' Union.

The conditions of the working class in Dublin at the time that Larkin arrived there were probably worse than in any city in Europe. Behind the splendour of the Georgian drawing-rooms, the dazzle of the Viceregal Court, the excitement of the literary revival, Dublin had this private shame. A priest appearing before a Government Commission in 1913 stated in evidence that he knew of a tenement house in which a hundred and seven people were living. According to the Medical Press in 1913 the death rate in Dublin was the highest in Europe, exceeding that of Moscow and even Calcutta where plague and cholera were rife. The conservative *Irish Times* in a leader in February 1914 compared the conditions in the Dublin slums to Dante's *Inferno*. Twenty-five thousand people were living in five thousand tenement houses, where over twenty thousand families lived in one room per family.

The two men who had selected this cess-pool for their reforming zeal were complementary in character. Larkin was a remarkable orator and journalist who could lift the people from their knees with a brilliant phrase. He had a voice that could carry across a prairie, and a towering, crag-like presence. His quivering face gleaming in the night as he roared his rhetoric to the crowds became the symbol of hope to the down-trodden and hungry masses who listened to him.

Connolly had not Larkin's gift of oratory or his extraordinary appeal to the masses but he did have a brilliant analytical mind that was capable of relating Marxist doctrine to Irish history and to conditions at that time. Connolly, the only Irish leader to have formulated a serious social policy, is regarded as a key figure in International Socialism. Like Larkin, he had been born outside Ireland, in Edinburgh, and was also of Irish parentage. After coming to Dublin, he had founded the Irish Socialist Republican Party which had adopted a motto of Camille Desmoulins, 'The great appear great because we are on our knees'. But this party had not prospered and Connolly had gone to America where he worked with Eugene Debs and the Syndicalists. Connolly had returned to Ireland in 1910 and become General Secretary of Larkin's Transport Union in Belfast the same year. Later in 1914, when Larkin went to America, Connolly was to take over his position in the Union and demonstrate his ability as a determined organizer and popular journalist.

Larkin was imprisoned in Sing Sing in 1916 and so missed the outbreak of the Rebellion the same year. When he returned to Ireland in 1923 after his release, the trouble was over and in his absence, Connolly (executed in 1916) had become a national martyr. But in 1913, it was Larkin who dominated the scene as he organized the first general strike in the world.

In the year 1913 in Dublin there had been thirty strikes between January and the middle of August. Then in that month, during the height of the Dublin Season which took place in Horse Show week, Larkin organized a transport strike. This was a direct challenge to his chief opponent William Murphy, a self-made man, who had built transport systems in many parts of the world, including South Africa. After Larkin had sprung the strike on him, Murphy accused the labour leader of infiltrating the delivery boy section of the *Irish Independent*, a national newspaper which Murphy also owned. His answer to Larkin was to lock out any employee of his paper who did not immediately resign from Larkin's Transport Union.

Larkin then persuaded the dockers not to handle goods coming to the firms who were distributors of Murphy's newspaper. This was an extension of his doctrine of 'tainted goods'. On September 3, the Dublin employers locked out twenty thousand men in an effort to break Larkin's Union and Dublin was in the grip of a strike that was to paralyse the city for six months. On Thursday, August 28, Larkin was arrested for seditious libel. Released on bail, he addressed a meeting of ten thousand people in Beresford Place near Liberty Hall, the headquarters of his Union. 'Before I go any further', he said, 'with your permission I am going to burn the Proclamation of the King. People make Kings and people can unmake them.'

He was due to speak in O'Connell Street on August 31, and fearing that there would be a warrant out for his arrest again, he went into hiding. The authorities made every effort to stop him appearing on that Sunday. Police guarded the entrances to all premises near the Imperial Hotel in O'Connell Street from which Larkin was due to address the crowd.

At half-past-one that Sunday an aged priest stepped out on the balcony of the Hotel and began to speak to the crowd. It was Larkin in disguise: the crowd soon recognized him and there was a roar of welcome before he was grabbed and taken away by the police. In the street below, a baton charge took place in which one man was killed and four hundred wounded. The police seemed to have behaved with calculated ferocity under the instruction of their officers who, in turn, had taken their brief from Dublin Castle.

In the next month the strike reached heights of bitterness. Socialists in the British Trade Unions sent over food ships to the strikers in Dublin. A plan was set up to send poor children to England to give them a holiday from the frightful conditions at home. The Catholic authorities objected. Pious protectors snatched the children from their parents' arms as they brought them down to the quays to the ship to take them to England. 'It's a poor religion that can't stand a fortnight's holiday', roared Larkin, released from jail, and as usual putting his finger unerringly on the hypocrisy which was reluctant to let starving children be given food and warmth for a few weeks.

During the strike Larkin was at his mightiest. He spoke in the Albert Hall, London, on the same platform as Bernard Shaw, to an audience of eight thousand. 'Hell has no terror for me,' he told them, 'I have lived there. Thirty six years of hunger and poverty have been my portion. They cannot terrify me with hell. Better to be in hell with Dante and Davitt than to be in heaven with Carson and Murphy.' Back in Dublin he unleashed more ferocious balaclavas on the employers, ending with the phrase 'They shall crucify Christ no longer in the streets of Dublin.'

Larkin's personality attracted the attention of many who were not aware of the plight of the Dublin worker before the strike began. Constance Markievicz was captivated by his personality and soon after she had met him was to be seen at the soup kitchen in the Labour headquarters, sleeves rolled up, ladling out soup to the hungry.

'Sitting there, listening to Larkin', she wrote later, 'I realized that I was in the presence of something that I had never come across before, some great primeval force rather than a man. A tornado, a storm-driven wave, the rush into life of spring, and the blasting breath of autumn, all seemed to emanate from the power that spoke. It seemed as if his personality caught up, assimilated, and threw back to the vast crowd that surrounded him every emotion that swayed them, every pain and joy that they had ever felt made articulate and sanctified. Only the great elemental force that is in all crowds had passed into his nature for ever . . . this force of his magically changed the whole life of the workers in Dublin and the whole outlook of trade unionism in Ireland.'

A. E. was another supporter. His 'Open Letter' to the employers written in October 1913 caused a sensation and was read and reread by workers in tenements throughout the city. 'The men whose manhood you have broken', he wrote in the *Manchester Guardian*, 'will loathe you, and will always be brooding and scheming to strike a fresh blow. The children will be taught to curse you. The infant being moulded in the womb will have breathed into its starved body the vitality of hate. It is not they – it is you who are blind Samsons pulling down the pillars of the social order. You are sounding the death knell of autocracy in industry. There was autocracy in political life, and it was superseded by democracy. So surely will democratic power wrest from you the control of industry. The fate of you, the aristocracy of industry, will be as the fate of the aristocracy of land if you do not show that you have some humanity still among you. Humanity abhors, above all things, a vacuum in itself, and your class will be cut off from humanity as the surgeon cuts the cancer and alien growth from the body. Be warned ere it is too late.'

The most important aftermath of the strike had been the formation of a Citizen Army in Dublin. After the police attack on the crowd on August 31, Larkin had urged the workers to form a militia for their own protection. As an example he cited the goings-on in Ulster. 'If it is right and legal for the men of Ulster to arm, why should it not be right and legal for the men of Dublin to arm themselves to protect themselves? You will need it. I don't offer advice which I am not prepared to adopt myself. You know me and you know that when I say a thing I will do it. So arm, and I'll arm. You have to face hired assassins. If Sir Edward Carson is right in telling the men of Ulster to form a provisional government in Ulster, I think I must be right, too, in telling you to form a provisional government in Dublin. But whether you form a provisional government or not, you will require arms.'

This army came into being in November 1913. Its constitution was drawn up by Sean O'Casey, who became Secretary of the Citizen Army and was to write its history. The Army Commander was Captain Jack White, D. S. O., an Antrim man and British Army Officer who had distinguished himself in the Boer War and was a son of Sir George White, defender of Ladysmith. Though White was later to resign his post, from the beginning he inculcated firm military principles into his 'Little Army' that were later to stand them in good stead and make the police less anxious to engage the workers in conflict than had previously been the case.

Shortly after he began his training programme, White received a telegram from Sir Roger Casement. 'I understand you begin movement to drill and discipline Dublin workers. This is a good and healthy movement. I wish to support it and I hope it may begin a widespread national movement to organize drilled and disciplined Irish Volunteers to assert Irish manhood and uphold the national cause in all that is right.'

White had met Casement at a nationalist meeting in Ballymoney and though they were fellow Antrim men and both Protestant nationalists, they had not liked each other on first meeting. Now White's defiance of the Government seems to have drawn Casement towards him. Both had served Britain with distinction and were now convinced that to oppose her was consistent with the principles which had led His Majesty to decorate them with high honours as soldier and diplomat.

The strike was the result of exploitation of Irishmen by Irishmen. But to many separatists it seemed merely another aspect of bad government brought about by the British presence in Ireland. Such conditions as pertained in Dublin could not have occurred in any other city in the British Isles. The strike was to draw people of separatist outlook together. Both the Citizen Army and the Irish Volunteers were to find their paths coming closer and closer until two years later they were both to form ranks and march as a unit to the centre of the city in open rebellion.

Chapter Eleven

The North under Carson was now virtually in a state of war. It was a challenge to democracy by an elite. Drilling took place daily and there were parades and marches through the streets of the main cities there. A motor cycle corps was founded and ambulance and Red Cross units in the formation of which ladies from aristocratic families played a leading part.

Then, in April 1914, a large consignment of arms and ammunition was landed at Larne in Bangor on the East Coast of Ulster. This included 24,600 rifles and 3,000,000 rounds of ammunition. They had been purchased secretly in Germany by a Colonel Crawford on behalf of the Ulster Volunteers.

Police and Customs officials who attempted to stop the illegal importation were physically threatened: as a result the authorities made no attempt to interfere with this brilliantly organized coup. On the night of April 6, hundreds of cars owned by the landed gentry were parked on all roads leading from Larne. These turned on their lights as soon as night fell so that the landing operation could take place with the maximum efficiency. Afterwards the cars stole off into the night with their illegal contraband and placed the arms in secret hiding places until they could be distributed to the mass of the Volunteers. It was the marshalling of a class in defence of its existence.

One consequence of the arming of the Ulster Volunteers had been that the Volunteers in the South should consider adopting a similar course. As a result of a series of meetings in London, it was arranged that arms would be purchased by Sir Roger Casement at Hamburg and dispatched to Ireland by boat.

In July 1914 a yacht set out from Hamburg loaded with 15,000 rifles and 100,000 rounds of ammunition, for the Irish Volunteers. Those on board were by any standards an unusual collection of people to be running arms for rebels. In charge of the yacht was Erskine Childers, a former Clerk in the House of

Commons and a nephew of a Chancellor of the Exchequer in Gladstone's cabinet. His wife, Molly Childers, who was also on board, had been born Molly Osgood and was a direct descendant of John Adams, the second President of the United States. The other man on board was Gordon Shephard, later to become the youngest Brigadier in the British Armed Forces and who was to die while serving in the Royal Flying Corps. On board also was Mary Spring Rice, daughter of Lord Monteagle and cousin of the British Ambassador in Washington.

When one adds that the arms had been purchased by a former British Consul and that the initial meeting of the Arms Committee had been held in the house of the middle-aged daughter of the Protestant Archdeacon of Meath, it will be seen that the importation of arms by the Irish Volunteers had a bizarre element that distinguishes it from most revolutionary undertakings.

One factor that this unusual group had in common was a determination that Parliament should not give in to armed threats from the right wing of the Conservative Party. Another ability they shared was that, being of upper-class background, they knew how to sail yachts. Childers in fact had written a yachting classic, *The Riddle of the Sands*, which had become a bedside book of almost every schoolboy of that generation.

Only yachtsmen of real skill could have brought the *Asgard* from Hamburg to Dublin unscathed that July. The yacht was in constant danger of interception by British destroyers in the North Sea. Childers refused to stop at the Isle of Wight for a clean-up and rest, arguing with some reason that the Volunteers would prefer to have their arms delivered by an unshaven and unwashed crew than have them captured by Crown forces on the Isle of Wight. The arms were finally landed from Childers' yacht at Howth peninsula about ten miles from Dublin on July 10, 1914. They were distributed immediately to waiting Volunteers who formed fours and marched into Dublin with them.

The Irish Volunteers, however, did not have as much luck as their Ulster counterparts. A number of them had managed to escape with their arms when they were stopped by the army on the Dublin road. But later on, a detachment of the Regiment who had confronted them (the King's Own Scottish Borderers),

61

opened fire on a crowd at Bachelor's Walk in the centre of the city, killing four people and wounding thirty-eight.

Chapter Twelve

Those who maintained that there was one law for the North and another for the South had their argument strengthened by the Batchelor's Walk affair. But an incident in the first week of May was to have such an effect on the public mind that it is arguable that some of its consequences are still felt today. This was a revolt within the citadel regarded as the final protector of the rule of law. It had never been doubted that the Army would carry out the orders of the Executive no matter how unpalatable these might seem to the officers concerned.

In March 1914, a Cabinet dispatch was sent to the Commander of the Army in Ireland, Sir Arthur Paget, asking him to detail detachments of troops to protect depots in Ulster which it was thought were in danger of being raided for arms by the Ulster Volunteers.

The effect of this was explosive and unprecedented. The majority of the officers at the Curragh (the military centre of Ireland) including the Commander of the Cavalry Brigade, General Sir Hubert Gough, made it known that they would resign their commissions rather than undertake military operations against the Ulster Volunteers. This was mutiny, no matter by what title those who wanted to reconcile the function of the Army and the authority of the Executive might want to call it.

This is no doubt that it was organized at Command level and that a conspiracy existed to force the hand of the Government if it should attempt to coerce Ulster. The leader of this sordid intrigue was General Sir Henry Wilson, the director of military operations in the Army at the time. Wilson was an Irishman from Fermanagh who had made up for his failure to pass his exams at Sandhurst by an acute sense of public relations and a willingness to impart confidential military information to those whom he thought might further his ends. A sinister figure flitting from Cabinet Minister to Leader of the Opposition, from his own intelligence department to the Ulster Volunteers, his activities foreshadow disturbing tendencies that were to have a disastrous effect on certain European nations after the war. Wilson and the members of his army conspiracy were in fact Europe's first Fascists.

The atmosphere in the Curragh Camp was electric. Churchill, as First Lord of the Admiralty, had despatched a flotilla of destroyers from the Irish Channel to deal with disturbances which were expected in Ulster. Were the officers to be called on to support this precipitate action? Would their desperate gamble to defy the Executive and at the same time retain their commissions succeed? One of the officers at the Curragh at that time, Lieutenant William Creagh, has described (in a letter to the author) how he was blackballed in the Curragh Officers' Mess, because he suggested that his fellow officers should consider writing to His Majesty before embarking on what would seem to him treasonable activities. As a result of his stand, Creagh's subsequent military career was affected.

At an emergency meeting, the Cabinet decided that, rather than risk large-scale defections from the Army Council, an assurance would be given to the mutineers that they would not be required in any operation against Ulster if it was decided to enforce the law against the parliamentary opposition there. Thus reassured, the officers returned to their Brigades and the Curragh incident was over.

The effect of what had happened, when it became known to the general public was to have a profound influence on the future of Irish politics. To many it seemed now that Parliament would compromise when faced with a threat of force. The Army High Command was dominated by a class who came from the landed aristocracy of Britain and Ireland and whose views were coloured by authoritarian beliefs. Simply they refused to execute laws in relation to their own class, that they would have approved when applied to others. Such a reaction was not unpredictable. During the first Home Rule debate Lord Salisbury had compared the Irish to the 'Hottentot and the Hindu' races who were not fit to govern themselves and Lord Roberts would not have felt that he was echoing beliefs foreign to his class when he wrote: 'However well educated and clever a native may be and however brave he may have proved himself, I believe that no rank that we can bestow on him could cause him to be considered an equal by a British Officer.'

A remarkable instance of an apparently high-minded future Prime Minister behaving, when it came to colonial affairs, in a manner that would make a Tammany boss blush is recorded by William Henry Joyce, an Irish Magistrate. Joyce had been employed by the British Government in Ireland to collect evidence to incriminate Parnell on conspiracy charges. In the course of examining official records Joyce came upon a document which seemed to conflict with the evidence they were going to present. He went to see Arthur Balfour, then Secretary of State for Ireland.

'He listened attentively to what I said. He was at the time standing in front of an open fireplace in which a fire was burning brightly. This was in his private office in the Castle. When I had finished he made a motion with his hands of tearing a document in pieces – then turning towards the fire he made a further motion to throw the fragments into the fire, he then faced me and nodded in a significant manner – all the time he said nothing. It is unnecessary to point out that this dumb pantomime was carried out with a view to indicating to me that I was to tear up the paper and burn it. I then left him, but the unpleasant incident produced an indelible impression upon my mind of the extraordinary psychological mentality of a powerful statesman (who was then in training to be Prime Minister of England) with regard to the destruction of inconvenient papers.'[1]

Thus was the devious charade by which an elite would maintain their position. In the last event they felt themselves above the law. They were abetted by what in another context has been regarded as the glory of the system – the absence of a Constitution. Under the canopy provided by this chosen ambiguity of a pragmatic people were a section of them able to shelter when confronted by the final demand of the Executive.

The Curragh Mutiny was the culmination of the refusal of the landed classes to recognize the rule of law where Ireland was concerned.

---

[1] *The Prime Informer* by Leon O'Broin – pp. 168–9.

Writing a month after it occurred, Lenin, with extraordinary prescience, recognized the significance of the event.

'March 21st 1914,' he wrote, 'will be an epoch-making turning-point, the day when the noble landlords of Britain smashed the British Constitution and British Law to bits and gave an excellent lesson in class struggle.'

It was the Curragh incident more than any event between 1912 and 1914 which turned people of moderate views towards revolutionary doctrines.

It was to have wide implications outside the Irish context. By this act of the Army in March 1914, the fabric of the Empire was rent; the prospect which high-minded people held of a community of nations evolving out of the Empire, joined together by bonds of race, tradition and law, was defeated, and the tortuous process begun by which nations sought their freedom through the bloody methods of revolution.

What was John Redmond's reaction to these significant events? The Home Rule Bill had passed the final stage in the Houses of Parliament on May 6, and was due to receive the Royal assent in September.

At this time, Redmond, to some extent, was isolated from the popular mind. He was understandably preoccupied with what was to be the culmination of his life's purpose. He would obtain for his countrymen the right to self-government which had been snatched from Parnell's hands when it was almost within his grasp. Redmond believed in the supremacy of Parliament and in its ultimate survival when faced with the forces of disorder.

He saw Irish affairs from Westminster rather than from the point of view of an Irishman living at home. He had given his reluctant approval to the formation of the Irish Volunteers only because he felt that if he had withheld it, he would have lost control of what was in his eyes a potentially dangerous organization.

It is interesting to speculate what might have happened if Europe had not been at war when the Home Rule Bill received the Royal assent in September 1914. Would Redmond's restraint have proved justified and Ireland been granted self-government before 1915? The probability is that this would have been the case, with certain temporary limitations on areas where the Act would immediately operate.

But by the time the Home Rule Bill was placed on the Statute Book, Britain and France were at war with Germany. A small country's aspirations for freedom within the Empire were soon forgotten, as in Churchill's words, 'this hateful issue was drowned in the cannonade of Armageddon'.

On August 3, Sir Edward Grey, in the House of Commons announced that from midnight of August 4 Great Britain would be at war with Germany. At this moment, Redmond was in a position of great strength. He had at his disposal a force of over 180,000 trained men. His authority at that time was such that he could have reduced the number of Irishmen who would have volunteered for the armed forces to a mere trickle if he had wished.

Had Redmond refused to allow recruiting among the Nationalist population and refused to co-operate with Britain until the Home Rule Bill was enacted, it is extremely unlikely that the Rebellion of 1916 could have taken place. The rebels by then would after all have been fighting against a Government constituted of Irishmen and it is unthinkable that in all the circumstances even the most hot-headed extremists would have agreed to such a course.

A year after the war started, Britain was desperate for manpower. If Redmond had held his 'troops' until then he would have had Home Rule for the asking. Instead on August 3, 1914, he made the mistake of committing the Irish Volunteers to the British cause without consultation with his party and without the support of many of his countrymen. It was a quixotic gesture, of the kind which Irishmen have often displayed towards Englishmen and as often the case, when the small behave chivalrously towards the mighty, was as effective in obtaining the ends it sought as a whistle in the wind.

'In the past', Redmond said in Parliament on August 3, 'when this Empire is being engaged in these terrible enterprises, it is true the sympathy of the Nationalists of Ireland for reasons to be found deep down in the centuries of history has been estranged from this country. Allow me to say so that what has occurred in recent years has altered the situation completely and today I honestly believe that the democracy of Ireland will turn with the utmost anxiety and sympathy to this country in every trial and every danger that may overtake it.'

Continuing, he recalled the support given by the Irish Catholics to the Irish Volunteers of the eighteenth century and said that the Government might withdraw all its troops from Ireland, the coasts would be defended 'by our armed sons and the national volunteers would gladly join in doing so with their brethren in the North'.

The enthusiasm which followed Redmond's chivalrous offer was immense. William Crooks, a Member of Parliament, called out 'God Save Ireland'. Redmond called out in reply, 'God Save England'. In the next few weeks, the Irish were the most popular people in the British Isles. Sir Edward Grey referred to Ireland as the 'one bright spot in the very dreadful situation'.

In gratitude the Home Rule Bill was placed on the Statute Book with the proviso that it should not come into operation until after the war.

Recruiting began immediately in Ireland and the results were remarkable. Irishmen flocked to the colours encouraged by their leaders in the belief that they were now fighting side by side with their old enemy for the freedom of small nations, and that Ireland would be one of these after the war.

Over 300,000 Catholic Irishmen fought in the Great War; about 40,000 of them were killed. They won more V.C.s between them – in proportion to the number of those fighting – than any other part of the Empire engaged in the war. Old established Irish regiments, the Munster Fusiliers, the Connaught Rangers, the Royal Dublin Fusiliers, the Leinsters, fought in the major engagements of the war. At Ypres, Gallipoli, Suvla Bay, the Somme, they upheld the tradition of Irishmen as excellent soldiers no matter for what cause they were fighting. 'Their persistency, their willpower, their physical endurance', wrote Churchill of the Dublin Fusiliers, the Munsters and the Hampshire Regiment at the assault of Sed-El-Bahr, 'achieved a feat of arms certainly in these respects not often, if ever, surpassed in the history of either island race.'

The streets of the Irish cities in the first years of the war were full of cheering crowds as the troops departed for France. Theatres put on war pageants, orchestras, in addition to the National Anthem, played 'Rule Britannia' as well. Smartly dressed newly-commissioned officers paraded Grafton Street with their girl friends. At the National University, the President, Dr Denis Coffey, shook each student by the hand as he went out to fight for King and country – the country in this case hopefully being regarded as Ireland.

Tom Kettle, the professor of National Economics at the National University, and 'the most brilliant mind of his generation' (according to Chesterton) resigned from the Faculty and his splendid figure clad in khaki could be seen recruiting throughout Ireland for Kitchener's Army. Kettle's action was typical of the euphoria of the time. Young men rushed to join the forces in case the war would end before they had a chance to show their gratitude to the old enemy by fighting side by side with her.

There were, though, some indications at this stage of the rigid attitude of the Army High Command towards Ireland that could have given Redmond's supporters twinges of uneasiness. It soon emerged that, despite their willingness to serve in the army, Catholic Irishmen would still be regarded as second-class citizens.

The Ulster Volunteers had been allowed to re-group themselves in a newly-formed Ulster Division. No such concessions were made to those in the South. Kitchener persistently refused to let an Irish Division be formed there. Lady Fingall, and her friend the Countess of Mayo, were actually embroidering a new flag for an Irish Brigade when they learned of Kitchener's refusal to allow it to be formed.

In the first years of the war, Irish Catholics found it difficult to get commissions in British regiments stationed in Ireland. Redmond's son, William, after being refused a commission in the Munster Fusiliers, applied to the Brigade of Guards where he was immediately commissioned.

Kitchener was suspicious of the Southern Irish. While he was quite prepared to use them as cannon fodder in military expeditions, he preferred to place his trust in Ulster Protestants who, a few months previously, had been negotiating with the

Kaiser as an alternative to accepting the authority of the British Crown.

Chapter Thirteen

In mid-September 1914, the Supreme Council of the Irish Republican Brotherhood met and decided that a rising would take place in Ireland before the end of the war. A Military Council was formed with Tom Clarke, Sean MacDermott and Joseph Plunkett. Later Thomas MacDonagh, lecturer in English at the National University, was co-opted on it. The purpose of the Military Council was to organize an insurrection as soon as possible. They were in contact with the revolutionary directors of Clann na Gael in New York who had promised to supply arms and money.

The Irish Volunteers were still, of course, under Redmond's control. But, on September 20, a tactless speech he made at Woodenbridge, Co. Wicklow, where he seemed to act in Arthur Griffith's words as 'a recruiting sergeant for Britain', created an immediate split in the Volunteer Movement. The result was that 170,000 went with Redmond while the remaining 10,000 stayed under Eoin MacNeill's control. This latter group were regarded by the Supreme Council of the I.R.B. as a nucleus from which a rebellion might be plotted.

From the beginning of hostilities, James Connolly had opposed the European war in the pages of the *Irish Worker*. As a Socialist, he had looked upon the struggle as a battle for markets and colonies between capitalist powers. 'I know of no foreign enemy in this country', he wrote, 'except the British Government. Should a German Army land in Ireland tomorrow, we should be perfectly justified in joining it, if by so doing we could rid this country once and for all of its connection with the Brigand Empire that drags us unwillingly to war.'

When the War began, Connolly had been primarily a Socialist with international views, while Padraic Pearse had been an Irish Separatist with a sense of social justice but without doctrinaire views. As 1916 approached, Pearse and Connolly began to draw close to one another from different directions. Connolly was later to say of his Socialist comrades in Europe, 'They will never understand what I am doing in the Rebellion because they will forget that I am an Irishman.' While Pearse was to write a few weeks before the Rising, 'Let no man be mistaken as to who will be lord in Ireland when Ireland is free. The people will be Lord and Master.'

Let us take a look at Pearse's school, St Enda's, in the year 1915. It is at Rathfarnham, high over Dublin, with gorse-covered mountains behind it, and in front the great sweep of Dublin Bay with Howth Head jutting out, the peninsula where the Scandinavian founders of Dublin had landed in the ninth century. There are massive stone gates outside the school, with carved lions lying on the ground. At the end of a long drive, there is a handsome classical mansion with stone pillars supporting the portico at the front.

Around the playing fields, pupils in saffron kilts are playing hurling, the ancient Irish game. They have elected to play this sport rather than cricket, for Pearse, though he dearly wanted the boys to choose the Irish game, allowed them to vote for the one of their choice. As they play, they speak in Irish for this is the official language of the school. Pearse's aim was to bring his pupils in touch with the ancient culture of Ireland in somewhat the same way as Thomas Arnold had inculcated the spirit of the Greek ideal among boys at Rugby School in the early nineteenth century.

Walking up and down the path in front of the Greek colonnade of the house are Pearse and some of the masters. Pearse's height singles him out from the others for he is over 6 ft.[1] One of them is Thomas MacDonagh, lecturer in English at the National University, another perhaps would be Joseph Plunkett, poet and editor of the *Irish Review*, the leading literary magazine of the time. Plunkett had been educated at an English public school, Stonyhurst, and speaks with an upper-class English accent. He

---

[1] Pearse's athletic appearance once led a Dublin crowd to mistake him for Jem Roche, the boxer, as he came out of the Dolphin Hotel. Roche was due to fight Tommy Burns the following day for the heavyweight championship of the world. Pearse was not at all taken aback and joined his hands and shook them over his head in the approved prize-fighter gesture in acknowledgement of the cheers of the crowd.

has been for health reasons to North Africa and brought back some of the habits of self-adornment that flourish in those countries. He wears large rings on his fingers.

All three are men of letters. Pearse's passions are for Shakespeare, Flaubert, Verlaine, Wordsworth, while Plunkett inclines to the mystical poets, St John of the Cross, St Francis, John Donne. MacDonagh is the scholar of the three, for he has published a widely-read book on the influence of early Anglo-Saxon metres in Irish poetry. He will argue for hours on his theory that quantity not stress is the real basis of English verse and that accent is relatively unimportant in English verse written by Irishmen.

When the conversation touches on Gaelic literature, Plunkett is not so much at ease with the other two. It is only lately that he has taken up the study of Irish under MacDonagh's tuition. But it is impossible for Pearse and MacDonagh to have a conversation without talking about Gaelic literature and comparing their most recent translations of poems translated from that language.

MacDonagh will probably remain on after the boys have gone into class, for he is a part-time teacher at St Enda's, but Plunkett will set out for the city in his motorcar. This is an unusual acquisition in the frugal atmosphere of drawing-room Dublin. But Plunkett can afford it because he has private means. Many of his nights he will spend at the theatre for he and MacDonagh and Edward Martyn have founded 'the Irish Literary Theatre' in order to bring before Dublin audiences plays of Ibsen, Strindberg, Shaw and Chekhov, in counterpoint to the Abbey Theatre's policy of presenting plays by Irish dramatists only.

Before they part from each other, the three men will have discussed the matter which is occupying them most at that time – the Rising against England. All three are members of the Military Council of the I.R.B. and are aware that the Rebellion is imminent.

Lest it be thought that the spectacle of poets in charge of a Rebellion against an Empire is an incongruous one, recall that it is the poets in the community who sense first stirrings in the national being. The sordid conspiracies that had emerged in the past four years had convinced Plunkett and MacDonagh as well as Pearse that Ireland was doomed unless she managed to extricate herself from England's grip.

Their main hope was that the British would enforce conscription and that the Nation might rally round in an attempt to resist it. If conscription did not become an issue, the Rising would be begun in any event in the hope that for a short period it would bring into existence an independent republic, and that on this basis a plea could be made for Ireland's case at the Peace Conference to be held at the end of the war.

Even if they failed, and they all three knew that an armed rising at the time in Ireland was likely to fail, they felt that they would have revived the soul of the Nation. 'We must be ready to die', Pearse wrote at this time, 'even as Emmet died on the gallows, as Christ died on Calvary, so that the people may live.' On the door of his school, Pearse had written the legend of the Irish hero Cuchulain, 'I care not that I live but one night and one day, if my deeds shall be remembered for ever.'

When the boys had gone to bed, the headmaster would return to his room to read chapters of his favourite book *The Tain*, which records Cuchulain's feats as told in the Irish Sagas. He would drink large quantities of tea out of an enormous willow-patterned cup; for he had sworn to drink only one cup a day and the large vessel was his device to keep his promise. In the sanctity of his study the only friend he welcomed was his brother, Willie, to whom he was devoted. They would talk far into the night, often breaking into brothers' private baby language. Willie was a sculptor and taught art at St Enda's. He and Padraic shared a love of the theatre and were fanatical admirers of Yeats. A short while before they went out in the Rising, they would produce some plays at Yeats' Abbey Theatre, Padraic helping Willie to distribute masks and costumes to the actors which his brother had designed.

Two years previously Yeats had selected Pearse's play, *An Ri* (The King) to present at the Abbey along with the first European production of Rabindranath Tagore's *The Post Office*. The highest compliment Yeats could pay to Tagore's school for Eastern boys was to call it 'the Indian St Enda's'.

The two brothers often referred to their father who had died some years before as 'The Governor'. James Pearse had been an

74

English sculptor who had come over to Dublin with Cardinal Newman to do the work for a new church in St Stephen's Green. Padraic used to say humorously about his father, of whom he was fond, 'Né ráibh sé ró olc mar Shasanach' (he wasn't too bad for an Englishman).

This is the Padraic Pearse who had earlier supported Redmond and who had spoken beside him in O'Connell Street at the mass meeting held to welcome Home Rule. What had changed his attitude in the meantime? The events surrounding the Curragh mutiny had certainly influenced him. Then his visit to America in 1914 to collect funds for his school and his meeting with John Devoy, head of Clann na Gael, had left him with the conviction that a revolution of some kind was necessary.

The poems Pearse wrote at this time envisage heroic action of some sort.

> I have squandered the splendid years:
> Lord, if I had the years I would squander
>   them over again,
> Aye, fling them from me!
> For this I have heard in my heart, that a
>   man shall scatter, not hoard,
> Shall do the deed of today, nor take thought
>   of tomorrow's teen,
> Shall not bargain or huxter with God; or
>   was it a jest of Christ's
> And is this my sin before men, to have
>   taken Him at His word?
> O wise men, riddle me this: what if the
>   dream come true?
> What if the dream come true? and if
>   millions unborn shall dwell
> In the house that I shaped in my heart, the
>   noble house of my thought?

In the summer of 1915 Pearse had gone to his cottage in Connemara to finish writing some short stories for children. He used these visits to the Irish-speaking part of Ireland, the Gaeltacht, as a means of renewal and to insulate himself against the spirit of the country at that time, which was wholeheartedly pro-British.

While he was in Connemara, he heard that he had been chosen to deliver the oration over the grave of O'Donovan Rossa, a Fenian Rebel who had died in New York and whose body was being brought back to Dublin. Pearse wrote the speech at short notice. But it is obvious now, however, that he intended to use the occasion to reaffirm the Republic tradition. 'This is a place of peace, sacred to the dead,' Pearse began at the graveside in Glasnevin Cemetery, Dublin, 'where men should speak with all charity and with all restraint: but I hold it a Christian thing, as O'Donovan Rossa held it, to hate evil, to hate untruth, to hate oppression, and hating them, to strive to overthrow them . . .'

Then he talked about the Revolutionary tradition and its influence on the present: 'Our foes are strong and wise and wary; but, strong and wise and wary as they are, they cannot undo the miracles of God who ripens in the hearts of young men the seeds sown by the young men of a former generation. And the seeds sown by the young men of '65 and '67 are coming to their miraculous ripening today. Rulers and Defenders of Realms had need to be wary if they would guard against such processes. Life springs from death: and from the graves of patriot men and women spring living nations.'

In his peroration Pearse actually went so far as to state his intentions in terms so explicit that it is hard to conceive how the authorities in Dublin Castle could have read them without taking action of some kind: 'The Defenders of this Realm have worked well in secret and in the open. They think that they have pacified Ireland. They think that they have purchased half of us and intimidated the other half. They think that they have foreseen everything, think that they have provided against everything; but the fools, the fools, the fools! – they have left us our Fenian dead, and while Ireland holds those graves, Ireland unfree shall never be at peace.[1]

In March 1916 Pearse as head of the Military Council received

[1] All Fenians had not offered to Rossa the unconditional worship that Pearse lavished on him. Writing in 1886 from New York to Matt Harris, Michael Davitt said: 'I have had to put up with that blatant ass Rossa who is doing damage here. He has not the courage to set fire to a British hay stack.'

a message from the revolutionary directorate of Clann na Gael in New York. 'Will send you 20,000 rifles, 10,000,000 rounds of ammunition to place near Tralee, between 22 and 28 of April.'

The poets were ready for action: and they were to have hearty encouragement from another, if somewhat surprising source.

James Connolly, independently of the Irish Republican Brotherhood, had decided to bring the Citizen Army out in rebellion before the War ended. On January 22, 1916, Connolly wrote in his paper, *The Workers Republic:*

> Mark well then our programme. While the war lasts and Ireland still is a subject nation we shall continue to urge her to fight for her freedom.
>
> We shall continue in season and out of season, to teach that the 'far-slung battle line' on England is weakest at the point nearest its heart, that Ireland is in that position of tactical advantage, that a defeat of England in India, Egypt, the Balkans or Flanders would not be so dangerous to the British Empire as any conflict of armed forces in Ireland, that the time for Ireland's battle is NOW, the place for Ireland's battle is HERE.

Fearful lest Connolly act precipitately and spoil the prospect of a concerted rebellion, the I.R.B. took Connolly to a meeting at a businessman's house in Crumlin, Dublin in January 1916. There he was told of the plans for a Rising. He also learned that Sir Roger Casement was in Germany, arranging the dispatch of arms for the rebel army. Connolly was delighted at the news and he and Plunkett talked long into the night discussing the tactics to be used in the Rising.

Plunkett was in charge of military strategy (he had gone to Germany on a secret arms mission in 1915) and it is an indication of his flair in these matters that Connolly did not demand any changes in the overall plan that was prepared. It was agreed that the Rising would begin on Easter Monday, 1916.

A few weeks after the Crumlin meeting, in the course of an English lecture at University College, Thomas MacDonagh to the surprise of the students took out a revolver and laid it in front of him on the desk. 'Ireland can only win freedom by force', he remarked, as if speaking to himself.

The students were dumbfounded. One of them, Austin Clarke the poet, who related the incident to the author, was especially surprised as the previous week MacDonagh had been trying to persuade him to do a thesis on the influence of Lute music on the shaping of the Tudor Lyric, a subject far removed from rebellion and the carrying about of revolvers.

Chapter Fourteen

The Easter Rising in Dublin began in confusion. The Commander-in-Chief of the Volunteers, Eoin MacNeill, had not been informed in advance of the plans. The Military Council of the I.R.B. had no intention of having him interfere with their carefully laid strategy. On Thursday, April 28, a notice appeared in the papers directing the Volunteers to mobilize for three days' manoeuvres at the Easter week-end. There was nothing unusual in this. The Volunteers frequently drilled at week-ends and Bank Holidays.

Late on Friday night MacNeill learned the true purpose of the manoeuvres. They were, in fact, a cover for a Rising which was to take place on Easter Monday. MacNeill was furious when he heard the news, and determined to stop the Rising at all costs. He went up immediately to St Enda's to see Pearse.

But the schoolmaster was adamant. The Rising would go on. He explained that German rifles and ammunition were due to arrive at Fenit in Co. Kerry that week-end. Much against his will MacNeill eventually agreed to allow the Rising to proceed on the grounds that if arms were to be distributed to the Volunteers the revolt would automatically start and it would lead to a greater catastrophe to cancel the arrangements.

Late on Saturday morning MacNeill learned that the arms had not arrived as planned. As a result of a misunderstanding between the Military Council and the German High Command as to the date of the arms landing, allied to the carelessness of the Kerry Commandant of the Volunteers, the arms ship had lain off County Kerry for three days awaiting orders to deliver its cargo. No contact had been made and the German captain scuttled his ship after it had been trapped by a British destroyer. Meanwhile, Sir Roger Casement, who had been in Germany since the beginning of the war as an envoy of Clann na Gael had landed on the south coast in a German submarine. Shortly after he landed he had been arrested by the local police.

MacNeill now felt that he had been thoroughly deceived by the Military Council.

One of his reasons for agreeing to allow the Rising to proceed had been his belief in the veracity of a document purporting to emanate from Dublin Castle which contained orders for the arrest of Volunteer leaders. Now MacNeill believed that the document was a forgery and that it had been 'planted on him'. He was determined to stop the Rising at all costs and inserted an advertisement in the Sunday newspapers cancelling the following day's manoeuvres. Pearse's answer to this was to send emissaries around the country to visit the different units rallying the Volunteers on a personal basis. He realized that now it would be difficult to rouse the rest of the country, but he was determined to go out in Dublin.

To his joy he found that Connolly was equally determined. At 11 o'clock on Easter Monday, both men met at the Citizen Army Headquarters at Liberty Hall. Pearse would be the Commander-in-Chief. Connolly would serve under him. The two of them stood there shaking hands, their faces bright with elation. Pearse was tall, with a Roman profile; he wore an up-turned military hat like a Boer Commander. Connolly was smaller, squat with a drooping moustache which gave him a judicial appearance, and wore highly polished leggings. He grasped Pearse's hand. 'Thank God we've lived to see this day.'

Professor Mahaffy, the Trinity College wit, once said that in Ireland the inevitable never happens but the unexpected often occurs. Who could have predicted that on Easter Monday, 1916, the two men at the head of the rebel army would be the son of an Englishman, and an ex-British soldier born in Edinburgh?

Easter Monday in Ireland and Britain is a Bank Holiday. Over the week-end, people leave the cities, knowing they have an extra day's holiday before their return to work the following week.

In Dublin the week-end of Easter 1916 had been a glorious one: throughout Saturday and Sunday, there had been a continual trek to the silver beaches which stretch for miles on either side of the city or to the mountains that encircle it like a rosary.

On week-days the Military brought colour and style to Dublin's fashionable Grafton Street as the officers, with jingling spurs and splendid red uniforms, sauntered up and down. But on Easter Monday, 1916, there was hardly an officer in the city. The majority were at the Fairyhouse races outside the city.

Had any of the military been back in Dublin during the morning, they might have noticed a number of young men with bandoleers and rifles on their shoulders hurrying through the streets towards the centre of the city. But even if they had been observed, few people would have paid any attention. Professor Eoin MacNeill's Irish Volunteers frequently mustered at week-ends.

But this time, though the citizens could not have known it, these men were marching to begin a rebellion in the heart of the second city of the Empire.

The Rising began officially at 12 noon when Pearse and Connolly led their newly merged detachment out of Liberty Hall towards Sackville Street which was about three minutes' walk away. Their intention was to occupy the General Post Office. This was a splendid Palladian building which dominated the widest street in Dublin. Just opposite it, Admiral Nelson stood aloft on his high pillar surveying the city through his one good eye.

Connolly and Pearse mustered their troops as they approached the Post Office. There would not be many people in the building on account of the Bank Holiday. The military guard was minimal and they were quickly disarmed. In less than half an hour, the army of the Republic was in possession of the Post Office. The Republican flag was hauled on the roof. It was green, white and orange. Green for Ireland, orange for their Orange brethren in the North, and White for peace between the two.

Commandant-General Pearse went to the front of the building and, standing under the splendid portico, between the massive pillars, read the Proclamation of the Republic. He began: 'Irishmen and Irishwomen: in the name of God and of the dead generations from which she receives her old tradition of nationhood. Ireland, through us, summons her children to her flag and strikes for her freedom.'

Then Pearse read the Declaration of Rights and referred to the six previous rebellions which had been undertaken in order to assert these rights. 'We declare the right of the people of

Ireland to the ownership of Ireland, and to the unfettered control of Irish destinies, to be sovereign and indefeasible. The long usurpation of that right by a foreign people and Government has not extinguished the right, nor can it ever be extinguished except by the destruction of the Irish people. In every generation the Irish people have asserted their right to national freedom and sovereignty; six times during the past three hundred years they have asserted it in arms.'

Civil and religious liberty were guaranteed, as well as the proclamation of a promise that the divisions between people of different religions in Ireland which had been fostered by imperialism would be resolved under the new regime.[1]

When Pearse went back into the building, he was confronted by a strange-looking figure who wore a bangle and jewelled rings. He was tall and spoke with a distinctly English accent.

This was his friend Joseph Plunkett, who hadn't seen any reason to discard his usual gear simply because he was in military uniform.

Plunkett was looking justifiably pleased as it seemed temporarily at any rate that his strategy for holding the city looked as if it would succeed.

His plan had been to take the centre of the town and occupy strategic posts which would control the entrances to the city. Had rebellion broken out in other centres throughout the country, the Dublin garrison would have been a vital link in the chain of command. Troops would have had to be deployed throughout Ireland and the capital could have held out against what would necessarily have been depleted forces for some time.

But now leaders in the G.P.O. realized that the countermanding order had acted as a deterrent to at least half the Volunteers. Many centres throughout the country hadn't known the Rising was on, and even when the news had trickled through there was confusion and inaction.

Under Plunkett's plan Commandant Edmund Daly had been assigned to the historic Four Courts, a beautiful eighteenth-century building designed by Richard Gandon where the barris-

[1] Just after the Proclamation was read a bowler-hatted citizen near the G.P.O. urinated outside a closed public lavatory, shouting 'now we have a Republic we can do what we like.'

ters had their chambers and the High Court sat. Across the river, Sean Heuston was in occupation of the Mendicity Institution. Almost in a straight line behind him, Commandant Eamonn Kent was in occupation of the South Dublin Union, a huge sprawling complex of buildings which occupied fifty-two acres. Captain John Connolly occupied the City Hall, only a few yards away from Dublin Castle.

On the south side, the most important post was held by Commandant Eamon de Valera at Boland's Mills, a large bakery which overlooked the roads from Dun Laoghaire port at which troops would most likely disembark.

Under de Valera was a detachment at Mount Street Bridge which was to have the greatest military success of the insurrection. Unlike Connolly, who had his socialism to urge him on, or Pearse with his mystical ideas, de Valera had no such spur to bring him to the barricades. He was a hard-working professor of mathematics in a girls' college. At thirty-five years of age he was in line for the Chair of Mathematics at the National University. He was married with five children and had nothing but the prospect of a pleasant academic existence stretching out in front of him.

What drove him then to the barricades? Perhaps a simple sense of duty. Once he had committed himself to a cause he would not ignore its implications. He had an almost stubborn sense of persistence and was quite without fear. (An opponent of de Valera once said to me, 'That old bugger doesn't know how to spell the word "fear".')

De Valera was not without a tinge of the romantic. He once told the author that as he was walking up Leeson Street from the University with 'Tommy' MacDonagh three weeks before the Rising, they both looked at a remarkable sunset and agreed that it was an omen for the event that was foremost in their minds that evening.

Thomas MacDonagh was in occupation of Jacob's biscuit factory. The lecturer at the National University had become a Commandant-in-Charge of a rebellion against the British Empire. A poem he had written to Pearse the year before could be a justification of his own position at this time.

His songs were a little phrase
    of eternal song,
Drowned in the harping of lays
    more loud and long.

His deed was a single work,
    Called out alone.
In the night when no echo stirred
    to laughter or moan.

But his songs new soul shall thrill
    the loud harps dumb.
And his deeds the echoes fill
    when the dawn is come.

At the far end of Grafton Street from O'Connell Street is St Stephen's Green. This is a large park surrounded on four sides by tall Georgian buildings. St Stephen's Green had been occupied by Commandant Michael Mallin of the Citizen Army. Like Connolly, Mallin was a socialist.

His Vice-Commandant was someone quite out of the ordinary. She wore a commando-style hat like Pearse and spoke with a high-pitched, upper-class English accent. She had a well-bred, aristocratic look, classical features and huge burning eyes. She gave orders to her soldiers rather in the manner of a mistress ordering her servants and unconsciously used Edwardian slang words. Yet among the men there was no one who did not worship her – the Countess Markievicz had arrived in Stephen's Green to join the Rebellion in her open car accompanied by two Fianna boys. The Fianna was a Sinn Fein version of the Boy Scouts, which the Countess had organized into a force after she had been disgusted by the sight of Baden-Powell scouts saluting the King in Dublin in 1908. Now as a senior officer in the Citizen Army, she had been given a command post in the Rebellion. She was a good shot, and carefully kept a tally of the number of Tommies whom she had brought down.[1]

[1] 'Con' Markievicz was to enter into the legend of the Dublin working class. Not long ago in a pub I saw a little old lady in her 70s get up and do a shuffling jig on the floor. She was barely able to lift her feet and explained her attenuated movements by saying that her 'tubes' were bad. She told us why she got up to dance. 'I was taught by the Countess.' For a second a presence lit the room.

The men in the battalion were devoted to the Countess, though they were conscious of her eccentricity. When one Volunteer stopped a car to commandeer it for a barricade, the Countess stepped up and shook the occupants by the hand; she had known them in her hunting days in the West of Ireland. She apologized for taking the car and explained it was to be used entirely for military purposes. Then she invited her friends to have a cup of tea before sending them on. The fact that she and her men were fighting for the extermination of the class she had invited to tea didn't seem to strike her as incongruous.

Chapter Fifteen

Back in the General Post Office, the Volunteers were breaking windows and erecting barricades around the four sides of the building. Outside the crowd seemed singularly unimpressed by what was taking place. They stole around the Post Office gaping idly at the young Volunteers who had their guns poked out through the broken windows and were resting on sandbags. In the hot Easter sun, it didn't seem like a rebellion at all.

'I met Stephen MacKenna (the translator of Plotinus) in the afternoon of Easter Monday', the poet, Austin Clarke, recalls. 'A restless, difficult crowd was gathered at the corner of Earl Street, while a few Volunteers armed with rifles and in full green uniform were endeavouring to keep order. As I made my way here and there through the scattered groups, I saw Stephen alone in a little space, lost in thought, indifferent to those about him. He was leaning weakly against a tram standard, but he greeted me in his quick melancholy way. He told me that he had hurried down that morning as soon as he heard the news. He had been there all day. He looked pale and ill; it was obvious that only the intensity of his own feelings and of the evening itself had sustained him. The G.P.O. was already cold grey in the shadow and beyond passing heads I could see again, almost obscured by the great pillars, the watchful figures of armed men behind the sandbagged windows. Clearly against the blue sky above the roof waved the flag of the Irish Republic declared that morning.

'Stephen MacKenna said little to me. Thought, emotion, could find no other end for themselves than the words "At Last". Certainly, neither of us mentioned any of those friends who, as we knew, must be at their posts, so near to us or somewhere else in the city.'

In the late afternoon the sentries in the Post Office observed a group of Lancers gathering at the far end of the street at Parnell's monument. The officers in the Post Office could see the plumes of the Lancers nodding as the horses pawed impatiently, anxious to start moving down the street. Presently Colonel Hammond gave the order to proceed. The horsemen rode up Sackville Street in faultless line, their pennants flying in the mild breeze.

Crash! A volley of rifle fire came from the G.P.O. Four Lancers lay dead on the cobble-stones. The rest broke up in disorder. The Colonel's arrogance had been responsible for sending his men into a situation which could only have resulted in death for some of them. Sealed in the security of his class, he never believed that rebels would actually fire on British troops.

Slowly, like a limb coming back to life after being deprived of circulation, the military command in Ireland were grasping the fact that they had a rebellion on their hands. The news had finally reached the Curragh at 12.30 p.m.; a naval wireless telegraph station had flashed the information to England.

Four thousand military were already on their way to Dublin from other parts of Ireland. Lord French, the Commander-in-Chief of the Home Forces in England, on hearing the news of the rebellion, immediately despatched the 59th Regiment to Dublin. Brigadier W. H. M. Lowe had been placed in charge of Crown Forces in the Dublin area.

In the G.P.O. Pearse and Connolly knew that the rebellion as they had envisaged it could not take place. The country was not with them as they feared and the rebel forces were grossly underarmed. The two leaders gave no indication to their men that they recognized the cause as hopeless; as they went from post to post laughing and chatting, it seemed to many Volunteers that it would not be long before the British were driven out of Ireland.

The following day, a heavy bombardment of the G.P.O. began. The British had brought a gunboat up the Liffey which commenced by shelling Liberty Hall. On Thursday morning, the gunboat directed its fire on the Post Office. A few guns were brought to the end of Sackville Street and commenced firing from there. By Thursday evening, it looked as if the whole of Dominick Street and Dorset Street to the north of the G.P.O. might go on fire. Abbey Street on the other side of the G.P.O. was also in flames. It became clear that General Lowe's policy was to concentrate on the G.P.O. and the Four Courts before proceeding to assign large detachments to the other resistance spots in the city. The Post Office was doomed. It was only a matter of time.

Connolly, seeking a new building to stage a last resistance, went out with a detachment to survey Abbey Street. He successfully sent his men into this street to occupy the Independent Newspaper building. Returning to the G.P.O. a ricochet bullet hit him in the ankle. In great agony, he crawled along the alleyway between Abbey Street and Princes Street and just managed to haul himself into the Post Office. A captured British Army doctor made a splint for the ankle and gave Connolly a shot of morphia to keep him out of pain for the night. In his sleep, he was heard to say as he lay groaning in the night, 'Has any man ever suffered as much pain for his Country?'

Meanwhile, Pearse walked round the G.P.O. recognizing that for the present the full responsibility of the Rising was on his shoulders. Connolly would not make decisions for some time. His face lit up by the shadow of the flames that were coming from outside the building, Pearse talked to one of the students from St Enda's who had come in to join the Rising. He laughed when the student told him how as they left St Enda's, Mrs Pearse admonished them: 'If you win this week boys, don't forget it was the son of an Englishman that freed you.' 'That's mother', was Pearse's comment.

He admitted now he was frightened by the bullets which rattled through the gaunt hall they were sitting in. 'Anyone who is not afraid of bullets is a liar', he said. He tried to look into the future to judge the effect of his actions on generations to come. 'When we are wiped out, people will blame us for everything and condemn us. But only for this protest, the war would have ended and nothing would have been done. After a few years, they will see the meaning of what we are trying to do.'

His imagination had been stirred by the actions of O'Rahilly, a Volunteer leader from Kerry. The day before the Rising, O'Rahilly, a Kerry magistrate, charged into Pearse's study in Rathfarnham with a gun, accusing him of trying to start the Rising without authority. Then he had left to go out and try and stop the Rising. Pearse had been surprised on the Monday when he saw a car drawing up to the G.P.O. and O'Rahilly jumping out. He had a smile on his face. 'I helped to wind the clock,' he said, 'I might as well see it strike.'

Pearse seemed to know that he and his fellow Volunteers were slipping into history. 'Emmet's two-hour insurrection is nothing to this', he said. 'They will talk of Dublin in the future as one of the splendid cities. Dublin's name will be glorious forever.'

Outside the General Post Office, Sean O'Casey walked the streets watching the destruction of the city and noting with his writer's eye events that would become part of history.

In the sky the flames were soaring higher, till the heavens looked like a great ruby hanging from God's ear. It was tinging the buildings like a scarlet glow, while the saints stretched their ears to catch the tenor of the Irish prayers going up, for each paternoster and ave maria mingled with the biting snarl from the Howth guns, and the answering roar from Saxon rifle, machine-gun, and cannon, that were weaving a closer cordon of fire round the Sinn Feiners, the fire creeping towards the group of innocent blessed with arms in their hands for the first time. Now it was above them, locking away the roof from over their heads, and they were too weary to go on trying to put it out. Their haggard faces were chipped into bleeding jaggedness by splinters flying from shattered stones and brick; the wounded were in a corner making their moan to themselves, while a few men and women were risking their lives to get the seriously hurt away to some hospital, wending their way through falling walls, fire and brimstone, and gauntlets of burning buildings. The grey-green Volunteer uniforms now no longer looked neat; they were ragged, and powdered thick with the pulverized mortar clouding from the walls. The fighters now looked like automatons moving unsteadily about, encased tightly in a fog of dust and acrid ashes. They were silent, unshaven, maybe muttering an act of contrition for things done before they went to war; wan-eyed, they persuaded their drooping lids to lift again, for drowsiness might mean a sudden and silent death to them. Those handiest with a rifle kept firing into the flames coming closer; a few, hoarse and parched, still tried to control the flames with tiny buckets of water, their leaders, before a wall of flame, standing dignified

89

among them, already garlanded for death; gay outwardly, and satisfied, their inner wakefulness wondering how they'd fare with the world faded. They had helped God to rouse up Ireland: let the whole people answer for them now? For them, now tired and worn, there was but a long, long sleep; a thin ribbon of flame from a line of levelled muskets, and then a long sleep. For evermore, Ireland's Easter lilies would have a crimson streak through them.

Oliver St John Gogarty watched the proceedings unconcernedly from the steps of his consulting rooms beside the Shelbourne Hotel in Stephen's Green. He cheerfully reminded George Moore who called on him from his house nearby in Ely Place, that the Rebellion could do the Empire nothing but good as it would redeem their credit in Europe, bringing them their sole current victory.

James Stephens who had spent the first part of the week walking round the city observing the attitudes of the people to the Revolution, as he went to bed on the Thursday noted how the silences alternated with the sound of artillery fire and bombs bursting.

This night also was calm and beautiful, but this night was the most sinister and woeful of those that had passed. The sound of artillery, of rifles, machine guns, grenades, did not cease even for a moment. From my window I saw a red flare that crept to the sky, and stole over it and remained there glaring; the smoke reached from the ground to the clouds, and I could see great red sparks go soaring to enormous heights; while always, in the calm air, hour after hour there was the buzzing and rattling and thudding of guns, and, but for the guns, silence.

It is in a dead silence this Insurrection is being fought, and one imagines what must be the feeling of these men, young for the most part, and unused to violence, who are submitting silently to the crash and flame and explosion by which they are surrounded.

Chapter Sixteen

On Friday, April 28, General Sir John Maxwell arrived to take command. He had been Commander-in-Chief in Egypt before being ordered to what must have seemed to him a distasteful post in Dublin. He was determined to put down the rebels with a firm hand and issued a no-nonsense proclamation the afternoon he arrived. He would not, he said, hesitate to destroy all buildings in the area occupied by the rebels and advised women and children who might still be there to leave immediately. Shortly after it became apparent that Maxwell's plan was to be put into effect with efficiency.

The G.P.O. was surrounded by artillery and machine guns. The roof had fallen in and fires started in different parts of the building. Connolly asked to be carried out to the front of the Post Office so that he might direct operations from there. Lying in a cot, he dictated his despatch. He was in great pain, but the knowledge that they had lasted so long without surrendering made his suffering bearable.

The first detachment now made their exit from the G.P.O. Led by O'Rahilly and Michael Collins, they set off down Henry Street, the street at the side of the General Post Office, intending to make for Williams and Woods, a building at the end of the street. Machine-gun fire wrecked the street and it was clear that few of those who had left would reach the place they had set out for.

Another escape route had to be found – Connolly, unable to walk, had to be carried on a field stretcher and was a sitting target for a sniper. Eventually, a dash was made through a side alley which brought the party which contained Pearse, Plunkett, Sean MacDermott and the injured Connolly to a house in Moore Street. Here, after a conference, the leaders made a decision at 12.45 p.m. They would surrender. A Volunteer nurse, Miss Elizabeth O'Farrell, was sent as an emissary to General Lowe.

At 2.30 p.m. Pearse surrendered to General Lowe outside the General Post Office. The rebellion was over.

But while the fighting at the G.P.O. had stopped, a number of the other command posts were unaware that Pearse had surrendered. After an extraordinary week against all the odds, Eamonn Ceannt and his Vice-Commandant, Cathal Brugha, had succeeded in holding out at the South Dublin Union. Michael Mallin was still in command of the Royal College of Surgeons to which he had retreated from his original post in St Stephen's Green. Eamon de Valera was with a large contingent of men at Boland's Mills and Thomas MacDonagh was entrenched in Jacob's biscuit factory.

The most successful military action of the week had been that of seven Volunteers under Captain Michael Malone who had held the canal area near Mount Street Bridge.

For three days, they had held back four British battalions. Perched in a vantage post over the road coming in from the port at Dun Laoghaire, they had inflicted heavy casualties on British troops. Finally, on Friday, the post was captured. Most of the garrison was dead, including Michael Malone.

Although de Valera had been only a few hundred yards away no detachments had been sent.

Now when the surrender order came in, there was some dispute about whether his men should surrender or not. Coming out of Boland's Mills, de Valera said gallantly to the officer who took the surrender: 'Shoot me if you will but arrange for my men.'

As he was being led away, he murmured to the crowd who were standing on the sidewalks to watch the rebels: 'Oh, if you'd only come out with knives and forks.'

After some argument, Mallin eventually surrendered in the College of Surgeons. His second-in-command, Countess Markievicz, was more reluctant than he to give in to the British. She spurned the offer of a lift in a motorcar which had come from one of the British officers.

'I shall march at the head of my men,' she said.

Four days later, the executions began. Fifteen of the leaders were shot by a firing squad. Seven of the executed men had signed the Proclamation: Thomas J. Clarke, Sean MacDiarmada, P. H. Pearse, James Connolly, Thomas MacDonagh, Eamonn Ceannt and Joseph Plunkett. Pearse was the first. At his court martial, he said: When I was a child of ten I went down on my knees by my bedside one night and promised God that I should devote my life to an effort to free my country. I have kept my promise . . . I assume I am speaking to Englishmen who value their own freedom, and who profess to be fighting for the freedom of Belgium and Serbia. Believe that we too love freedom and desire it. To use it is more desirable than anything else in the world. If you strike us down now we shall rise again and renew the fight. You cannot conquer Ireland; you cannot extinguish the Irish passion for freedom; if our deed has not been sufficient to win freedom then our children will win it by a better deed.'

In a letter to his mother written the morning of his execution, Pearse said, 'This is the death I should have asked for if God had given me the choice of all deaths – to die a soldier's death for Ireland and for freedom. We have done right. People will say hard things of us now, but later on will praise us. Do not grieve for all this but think of it as a sacrifice which God asked of me and of you.'

He sent her a poem which he had written about a mother who would lose two sons: in the frenzied atmosphere of revenge that seemed to inspire the military that Easter Week, Pearse's brother, the sculptor, Willie, had been sentenced to die presumably because he had signed some mobilization orders as Acting Commandant General. (This poem hangs over Mrs Rose Kennedy's bed.)

> I do not grudge them; Lord, I do not grudge
> My two strong sons that I have seen go out
> To break their strength and die, they and a few,
> In bloody protest for a glorious thing,
> They shall be spoken of among their people,
> The generations shall remember them,
> And call them blessed:
> But I will speak their names to my own heart
> In the long nights;
> The little names that were familiar once

Round my dead hearth.
Lord, thou art hard on mothers;
We suffer in their coming and their going;
And tho' I grudge them not, I weary, weary
Of the long sorrow – And yet I have my joy;
My sons were faithful, and they fought.

Thomas MacDonagh was executed the next day. He told the court martial: 'You will, perhaps, understand this sentiment, for it is one to which an Imperial poet of bygone days bore immortal testimony: "'Tis sweet and glorious to die for one's country." You would all be proud to die for Britain, your Imperial patron, and I am proud and happy to die for Ireland, my glorious Fatherland . . . The Proclamation of the Irish Republic has been adduced in evidence against me as one of the signatories; you think it already a dead, a buried letter, but it lives, it lives. From minds alight with Ireland's vivid intellect, it sprang; in hearts aflame with Ireland's mighty love, it was conceived. Such documents do not die.'

The next to be shot was Plunkett. With his rings and earrings in the smoke of the Post Office, he had looked a figure from an Aubrey Beardsley painting. Now his death was to take on an exotic quality, as if he was living out some story written by a Florentine of the Quattrocento. The night before Plunkett's execution, a beautiful young girl was brought into the prison chapel. There, under the light of a candle, she was married to Plunkett by a priest. She was given ten minutes alone with him before he died. Her name was Grace Gifford. She was a young Protestant girl of good family and a talented artist, who had been Plunkett's fiancée for a year before the Rising. Now he gave her, as a memento, the text of a poem he had written out in his own hand, which had appeared in his book of poems published before the Rising.

I see his blood upon the rose
And in the stars the glory of his eyes,
His body gleams amid eternal snows,
His tears fall from the skies.

I see his face in every flower:
The thunder and the singing of the birds
Are but his voice – and carven by his power
Rocks are his written words.

All pathways by his feet are worn
His strong heart stirs the ever-beating sea,
His crown of thorns is twined with every thorn,
His cross is every tree.

Commandant Daly, Michael O'Hanrahan and Willie Pearse
were shot with Plunkett. Major John MacBride, husband of
Yeats' beloved Maud Gonne, was shot on May 5; then on May
8, Ceannt, Mallin, Heuston and Colbert were shot.

James Connolly had been court-martialled sitting in a chair.
He was still unable to get up because of his shattered ankle and
was in great agony. On May 11, he learned he was to be executed
with Sean MacDermott. A few minutes before he died he joked
with his wife and daughter, 'You know, Lily, a man came into
the General Post Office to buy a penny stamp. When he couldn't
get one he was most indignant and said "I don't know what
Dublin is coming to when you can't buy a stamp in the Post
Office".'

Katherine Tynan, the poetess, has left a description of Connolly's death as it was related to her by Surgeon Richard Tobin
who had been called in to attend to the wounded rebel.

'Can I do anything for you, Connolly?'

'I want nothing but liberty.'

'You must go to the Shan Van Vocht for that. Can I do
anything to make you easier?'

'What do you think will happen to me?' asked Connolly.

'You'll be shot.'

'Oh, you think that?'

'I am sure of it.'

'Why?'

'They can't do anything else. Can they buy you?'

'No.'

'Can they frighten you?'

'No.'

'Will you promise if they let you off with your life to go away and be a good boy for the future?'

'No.'

'They can do nothing else but shoot you.'

'Oh, I recognize that,' said Connolly.

Surgeon Tobin described to Katherine Tynan what happened just before Connolly was executed. His doctor, the indomitable Great-Heart, who had been in the King's service and held his fealty to the King to the end, said to the rebel who was about to die:

'Connolly, will you pray for the men who are about to shoot you?'

He turned a sudden beaming smile on the soldiers.

'I pray for all brave men who do their duty according to their lights,' he answered.

Connolly had to be carried to the execution yard. He was unable to stand up because of his wounds so they shot him sitting in his chair.[1]

As the remnants of the Volunteers walked down the Quays to imprisonment in England, working-class people hurled garbage at them. The air was thick with abuse. The Rebellion was denounced by the Nationalist establishment, the Church and the merchant classes. A few weeks later, the first few sparks began to kindle a flame that would grow into a furnace before the decade was over. Pearse was right. The people could be woken up if there were those who were ready to die for the country.

About 1,351 people had been killed or severely wounded in Easter Week. Most of the centre of Dublin was in ruins. Yet the Rising had remarkably little effect on the daily life of the city. The citizens had golfed, swum or played tennis only a mile or two from where the fighting was taking place.

Outwardly the sun shone through Georgian squares as it had done before the Rising. But a chemistry was at work which was to affect not only life in Dublin at the time but the quality of life throughout the British Empire and the other great powers who ruled the world at that time. The Dublin Rebellion was the

---

[1] Monk Gibbon, writer and poet, commented on this with Swiftian irony, 'Connolly was afforded the amenity of a chair so that he could be shot sitting up.'

1a. Charles Stuart Parnell. Photograph taken in Kitty O'Shea's house at Eltham in 1885

1b. John Redmond, leader of the Irish Parliamentary Party at Westminster, photographed at the time of the introduction of the Home Rule Bill in 1912

2. Constance Markievicz at the time of her presentation at Court

3a and 3b. Maud Gonne.
She was the inspiration
of Yeats' finest love poems
and introduced him
into the heart of the
revolutionary movement

4. Jim Larkin in full cry, Dublin 1913

5. National Executive, Irish Trade Union Congress and Labour Party, 1914.
Standing James Connolly, William O'Brien, M.J. Egan, Thomas Cassidy, W.E. Hill
and Richard O'Carroll. *Sitting* Thomas MacPartlin, D.R. Campbell, P.T. Daly,
James Larkin and M.J. O'Lehane

6a. The meeting of the Ulster Unionist Council at Belfast on
23 September, 1912. *Left to right* The Rt. Hon. J.H. Campbell,
Sir Edward Carson, Lord Londonderry (6th), Viscount Castlereagh
(7th Marquess of Londonderry), Mr. J. Craig (Lord Craigavon) and
Lord Willoughby de Broke (19th)

6b. Sir Edward Carson,
September 1913

7. Patrick Pearse, aged 18

8. Patrick Pearse's father, mother and sister. Pearse's father was an English sculptor from Cornwall who came to Dublin to work on the sculpture for Cardinal Newman's church in Stephen's Green. *Back left* Willie Pearse, Patrick's brother. Both brothers were executed after the Rebellion in 1916

9. Thomas MacDonagh on the Strand, summer of 1915. Poet and lecturer
in English at University College, Dublin, he was one of the
signatories of the Proclamation of Independence in 1916. He was
executed in May 1916

10. Countess Markievicz in the cast of *The Devil's Disciple* presented
at the Gaiety Theatre, Dublin, May 1913. The Countess is in the centre
sitting beside Count Casimir Markievicz, her husband,
who produced the play. She has a cocker spaniel on her knee

11a. A group of British officers under the Parnell monument
after the 1916 Rebellion. They are holding a captured flag,
thus appearing to give the rebels belligerent status

11b. Sackville Street after the Rising, May 1916.
The Dublin public viewing the damage

12. The German Submarine U.19 on which Roger Casement left
Heligoland to reach Tralee Bay. Casement, hatless and without
beard, is in the centre of the group in the conning tower

13a. Roger Casement
in his thirties

13b. Thomas Ashe, whose
death on hunger strike in 1917
was the event around which
the Volunteers reorganised
their forces

14a. Arthur Griffith and E.J. Duggan, October 1921

14b. Captain Jack White, D.S.O., Commander in Chief of The Citizen Army

15 .Michael Collins as a young man in the uniform of the Irish Volunteers

15b. Michael Collins at Arthur Griffith's funeral

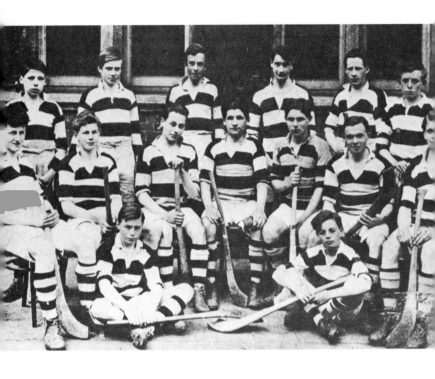

16. Kevin Barry *(seated third from left)* in the Belvedere hurling team, 1919. He also played rugby for the Belvedere first fifteen. Seated on the ground *(left)* is Eugene Davy, later to become one of the great rugby players of all time

17. Members of Michael Collins' 'Squad'. Their work was the elimination of secret agents who were attempting to capture Collins and his staff and paralyse the guerrilla resistance. *Left to right* Joe Leonard, Joe Slattery, Joe Dolan, Gearoid O'Sullivan, William Stapleton and Charlie Dalton

"THE RESOURCES OF CIVILISATION."

Mr. Lloyd George. "STICK TO IT, BONAR. POOR OLD SISYPHUS NEVER HAD AN IMPLEMENT LIKE THIS."

18. Cartoon from *Punch*, 20 October, 1920

19. A group of Auxiliaries, Dublin 1920

20. Black and Tans in Limerick.
Emerson and Lindsay were marked down for execution by the I.R.A.

21. Members of the Igoe Gang. These were a group of police spies under the leadership of a fearless R.I.C. officer, who were brought in from Country posts to identify Volunteers who would come in from Command post in the country to visit Headquarters in Dublin

WORTH A TRIAL.

ULSTERMAN. "HERE COMES A GIFT-HORSE FOR THE TWO OF US. WE'D BEST NOT LOOK HIM TOO CLOSE IN THE MOUTH."

SOUTHERN IRISHMAN. "I'LL NOT LOOK AT HIM AT ALL."

ULSTERMAN. "OH, YOU'LL THINK MORE OF HIM WHEN YOU SEE THE WAY HE MOVES WITH ME ON HIS BACK."

22. Cartoon from *Punch*, 17 November, 1920

23a. Eamon de Valera returns to Ireland
surrounded by a bodyguard, July 1921

23b. Arthur Griffith and
Eamon de Valera in London,
for de Valera's meeting
with Lloyd George
in July 1921

24. The funeral of British agents shot on Bloody Sunday.
Auxiliaries and Police form the guard of honour

beginning of the disintegration of Imperialism, the initiation of a pattern which was to repeat itself in India, Cyprus, Palestine and Egypt, Malaya, Kenya and Algeria. Dublin's well-bred young ladies, as they took out their parasols a few weeks after the Rising, to go to the College Races at Trinity College, could not have known that their way of life was threatened and would never be the same again.[1]

[1] The day after Connolly's execution George Bernard Shaw wrote to the *Daily News*:

Sir,

You say that 'so far as the leaders are concerned no voice has been raised against the infliction of the punishment which has so speedily overtaken them'. As the Government shot the prisoners first and told the public about it afterwards, there was no opportunity for effective protest. But it must not be assumed that those who merely shrugged their shoulders when it was useless to remonstrate accept for one moment the view that what happened was the execution of a gang of criminals.

My own view – which I should not intrude on you had you not concluded that it does not exist – is that the men who were shot in cold blood after their capture or surrender were prisoners of war, and that it was, therefore, entirely incorrect to slaughter them. The relation of Ireland to Dublin Castle is in this respect precisely that of the Balkan States to Turkey, of Belgium or the city of Lille to the Kaiser, and of the United States to Great Britain. The shot Irishmen will now take their places beside Emmet and the Manchester Martyrs in Ireland, and beside the heroes of Poland and Serbia and Belgium in Europe; and nothing in heaven or earth can prevent it.

Chapter Seventeen

'O words are lightly spoken,'
Said Pearse to Connolly,
'Maybe a breath of politic words
Has withered our Rose Tree;
Or maybe but a wind that blows
Across the bitter sea.'

'It needs to be but watered,'
James Connolly replied,
'To make the green come out again
And spread on every side,
And shake the blossom from the bud
To be the garden's pride.'

'But where can we draw water,'
Said Pearse to Connolly,
'When all the wells are parched away?
O plain as plain can be
There's nothing but our own red blood
Can make a right Rose Tree.'

                                   W. B. Yeats

The poets, very soon after the Rising, like Druids divining omens, began to scrutinize it in verse. Yeats, James Stephens, Lady Gregory, A.E., and Padraic Colum, wrote passionately against the executions, at the same time anticipating the effect the deaths of the leaders would have on the community.

Yeats is the hierarchic figure wandering around the Georgian streets in the Dublin gloom, wrapped in his cloak, allowing the meaning of the cataclysm to soak into his being as he observed it through the people he met. He remembered Pearse as:

This man had kept a school,
And rode our winged horse.

MacDonagh was:

> His helper and friend,
> Was coming into his force
> He might have won fame in the end
> So sensitive his nature seemed
> So daring and sweet his thought.

Yeats recognized now that he had failed to fathom the force the leaders contained within them. He had even despised some of them; meeting them going to work in the mornings they had seemed impracticable dreamers. Now he recognized that they had succeeded in changing the fabric of life under the 'grey eighteenth-century houses'.

> I write it out in a verse
> MacDonagh and MacBride
> And Connolly and Pearse
> Now and in time to be,
> Wherever green in worn
> Are changed, changed utterly:
> A terrible beauty is born.

Yeats' friend George Russell recognized that though he disagreed with the Rebellion in principle, a change would take place in the public attitude to it.

> Here's to you, Pearse, your dream, not mine
> But yet the thought – for this you fell –
> Turns all life's water into wine.
> I listened to high talk from you,
> Thomas MacDonagh, and it seemed
> The words were idle, but they grew
> To nobleness, by death redeemed.

James Stephens had been in Dublin during the Rising and had walked, fascinated, visiting the different command posts, talking to the men there whom he knew. 'If freedom', he had written in his journal, 'is to come to Ireland, as I believe it is, then the Easter Insurrection was the only thing that could have happened. We might have crept into liberty like some kind of domesticated man, whereas now we may be allowed to march into freedom with the honours of war.'

After the Rebellion, James Stephens was the first to hail the leaders with his poem 'Remembrance'.

> Be green upon their graves, O happy Spring!
> For they were young and eager who are dead!
> Of all things that are young, and quivering
> With eager life, be they remembered!
> They move not here! They have gone to the clay,
> They cannot die again for liberty.
> Be they remembered of their land for aye!
> Green be their graves, and green their memory!

Lady Gregory, cut off from her beloved Abbey Theatre during Easter Week, and losing one of her leading actors, Sean Connolly (who had been killed at City Hall), immediately recognized the significance of the week's events.

> In Easter Week the wisp was lit
> Waked Dublin from her drowsy years:
> I moan the battle anger, yet
> What did we ever win by tears?
> The ballad singers long have cried
> The shining names of far-away;
> Now let them rhyme out those that died
> With the three colours, yesterday.

Lady Gregory was right about the ballad singers.

Soon under the street lamps at night, as the customers emerged from the pubs, they would see the balladeers handing out broadsheets as they sang, the age-old method of the Irish for preserving the memory of lost battles.

> I had a true love, if ever a girl had one
> I had a true love, a brave lad was he
> One fine Easter Monday with his gallant comrades
> He started away for to set old Ireland free.
>
> All round my hat I'll wear a tri-coloured ribbon-o,
> All round my hat until death comes to me
> And if anybody asks me the reason I am wearing it
> I'll say it's for my true love I never more will see.

Less predictably, from the trenches in France came verse written by Irishmen who had joined the British Army to fight for the 'freedom of small nations'. Now they learned that their fellow poets in Dublin had been executed by soldiers of the army whose uniform they were wearing.

Professor Tom Kettle, a friend of James Joyce (he married Joyce's first girl-friend, Mary Sheehy) and a Lieutenant in the Royal Dublin Fusiliers, had asked for a transfer to the front line as soon as he heard of the executions in Dublin. Many of the dead men had been his friends. Believing that the Hun menace would destroy French civilization Kettle had recruited throughout Ireland before joining up himself. Soon after his transfer, Kettle was killed at Ginchy on the Somme. Shortly before his death he had sent back to his wife a sonnet he had written for their daughter. Its concluding lines expressed the disillusion of many Irish nationalists fighting in the trenches at that time.

> Know that we fools now with the foolish dead
> Died not for Flag nor King nor Emperor
> But for a dream born in a herdsman's shed
> And for the secret scriptures of the poor.

One wonders if the verse written after the Rebellion ever passed before the eyes of the politicians. They had missed the significance of the Rising. They could have found it in the poetry had they troubled to glance at it. There it was writ plain. But those who shape the destiny of empires pay little heed to poets; their eyes are fixed on horizons far beyond the hills and hedges of a small island on the edge of Europe struggling to regain its identity while great nations held each other in a death grip.

Chapter Eighteen

Though fifteen leaders had been shot by the middle of May, the execution of one was delayed. He was to have the formality of a judge and jury. The prisoner was a Commander of the Order of St Michael and St George and had as well been the recipient of a knighthood. It would be a show trial: he was charged with Treason, the gravest crime on the Statute Book.

Sir Roger Casement had left Ireland for America on July 14, shortly before the outbreak of war. In his last two years in Ireland he had thrown himself into the national movement. He had received a knighthood from the King in 1911 and shortly afterwards retired from the Consular Service on the grounds of ill health. Casement travelled about the country, organizing Gaelic League clubs and recruiting for the Irish Volunteers. He contributed articles and poems to the literary magazines. Padraic Colum, the poet, and an editor of *The Irish Review*, remembers Casement coming into his office with 'the appearance and manner of a Hidalgo and talking in a low, unforgettable voice of an impending crisis.'

Once on a trip through an impoverished part of Donegal, Casement had come across a young widow with a child living in a cabin. Later that evening Casement, still the Proconsul, gave the local parish priest, Canon McFadden, five pounds to buy a cow for the widow woman so that 'she always would have milk for her child.'[1]

Casement had also been involved in the plans to run guns for the Volunteers at Howth. Darrell Figgis, one of the organizers of the escapade, has left a vivid picture of Casement's reaction when the question of the guns was first raised in the house of Alice Stopford Green, the historian and Casement's friend in London. 'His face was in profile to me, his handsome head and noble outline cut out against the lattice work of the curtain and

[1] Told to the author by Professor Alphonsus O'Farrelly.

grey sky. As I spoke he left his place by the window and came forward towards me, his face alight with battle. "That's talking", he said, throwing his hands on the table between us.'

(There is a curious link between Figgis and Casement. T. E. Lawrence thought Figgis' novel *The Children of Earth* the finest of its time, while according to Bernard Shaw, Lawrence attempted to write the life of Casement but relinquished the idea when the British Government had refused to release the Casement papers.)

In July 1914, disgusted by Redmond's attempt to get control of the Volunteers, Casement had set out for New York. There he met John Devoy, the Fenian head of Clann na Gael and the key figure among the Irish groups in the United States. Casement was well received in America. 'They see me as a sort of aged Parnell', he wrote. 'I can see from the way they greet me that they are setting their hearts on a Protestant leader, and think, poor brave souls, I may be the man'.

While Casement was in the United States war broke out. He wrote a letter from New York to the *Irish Independent* setting out what he thought should be the attitude of Irishmen to the conflict. 'Our duty as a Christian people is to abstain from bloodshed; and our duty as Irishmen is to give our lives for Ireland. Ireland needs all her sons . . . Were the Home Rule Bill all that is claimed for it, and were it freely given today, to come into operation tomorrow instead of being offered for sale on terms of exchange that only a fool would accept, it would still be the duty of Irishmen to save their strength and manhood for the trying tasks before them, to build up from a depleted population the fabric of a ruined national life.'

While these were strong views, they did not express Casement's full feelings about the War. In his disquiet at the British Government's attitude towards Ulster and aligned with his own treatment at the hands of the Foreign Office bureaucrats, he had become a fanatical pro-German. The I.R.B. in Dublin and indeed Devoy's group in New York were not specially pro-German. If they could use the conflict as a means of furthering Ireland's cause, they were prepared to do so, even to the extent of accepting German help. Casement seems to have developed an obsession in this period which resulted in a glorification of German virtues to an extent that borders on the neurotic. There is evidence that he had become a prey to obsessions resulting from ill health, frustration at the Foreign Office, and his loathing for the British treatment of Ireland.

After negotiations with the German Ambassador in Washington, Casement persuaded Devoy to send him to Berlin as 'an envoy of the Irish Republic'. Landing in Germany in December 1914, Casement was to spend two futile years shunting backwards and forwards between different departments of the German Foreign Office. In the end he was to discover that one Foreign Office was much the same as another.

Disenchanted with Germany, and believing that help which was expected for the proposed Rising in 1916 in Dublin would not be forthcoming from the German General Staff, he had decided to return to Ireland by submarine to inform the leaders of the Rebellion of what he regarded as 'German treachery'.

After a difficult voyage, the submarine U19 surfaced in Tralee Bay on the south coast of Kerry on Holy Thursday 1916, three days before the Rising. Owing to a miscalculation there were no signals to bring Casement to land; so that he and two companions were sent ashore by the U-Boat captain in a canvas canoe while the submarine slid off into the Atlantic dawn.

In the heavy seas the canoe overturned and Casement barely managed to reach the shore. Exhausted and ill from the journey and wet from the sea, he took shelter in a fort while his companions set out to get aid. Later that morning he was discovered by a policeman out for a spin on a bicycle who arrested him and brought him to the Royal Irish Constabulary barracks in Tralee. From there he was taken to the Tower of London where he was held awaiting trial.

Chapter Nineteen

When a relative, Gertrude Bannister, went to visit Casement in the Tower of London, she found her cousin in filthy conditions. His clothes had not been changed since he had been arrested in the fort and they were sand stained and stiff with salt water. His prison bed was verminous and his body was covered in bites. Casement's friend, Alice Stopford Green, immediately she heard of his plight brought the matter to Asquith, and Casement was transferred to Brixton where he received reasonable treatment.

George Gavan Duffy, an Irish solicitor practising in London, agreed to take instructions for the defence. Despite the tradition of the English Bar that a barrister should not turn down a case if an adequate fee is offered, no one could be found to defend Casement. High Treason was the charge and the Bar apparently wanted no hand in it.

Eventually, Gavan Duffy contacted his brother-in-law, Serjeant Sullivan, a leader of the Irish Bar. Sullivan had been called as a young man to the English Bar and was, therefore, entitled to plead in Court for him in London. The title had gone out of use in England but was still employed in Ireland where it indicated that Counsel had once been briefed by the State.

Sullivan agreed to defend the case if he was offered a generous fee. This was procured and he arrived in England to interview his client. A less suitable person than Sullivan to conduct the defence could hardly be imagined. Casement was to be tried for High Treason and for suborning the loyalties of Irishmen in the British Army who were prisoners of war, by trying to get them to fight against England. Sullivan on the other hand had recruited actively for the British Army in Ireland and had publicly declared himself opposed to the Rising. He was a clever man but capable of much bitterness. The author can remember the bent figure of Serjeant Sullivan hunched in his legal gown hurrying in to law dinners at the King's Inns, Dublin. Sullivan was then ninety-one and as a Bencher of the King's Inns, he was entitled to preside with other Benchers at dinner. Shortly afterwards the Benchers took the unprecedented step of removing him from membership because he had disclosed to a journalist matters which were revealed to him by Casement in his relationship as client to barrister. Nearly forty years after the trial he was still incapable of concealing his dislike of his famous client.

At first Casement had resisted the suggestion that he brief Counsel. He wanted to plead guilty and tell the Court that as an Irishman he didn't recognize their jurisdiction over him. Quite independently of Casement's stand (which he was not aware of), Bernard Shaw had decided that it would be useless for the prisoner to take part in what must turn out to be a charade, and that he should insist that he was an Irishman and therefore not capable of Treason towards England. Shaw had even gone so far as to write out a speech for Casement, which ended, 'I am neither an Englishman nor a traitor; I am an Irishman captured in a fair attempt to achieve the independence of my country; and you can no more deprive me of the honours of that position, or destroy the effects of my efforts, than the abominable cruelties inflicted six hundred years ago on William Wallace, in this city, when he met a precisely similar indictment with a precisely similar reply, have prevented that brave and honourable Scot from becoming the national hero of his country.'

When Casement heard that Shaw's views coincided with his own, he was naturally delighted and asked Gavan Duffy to convey to the Irish dramatist 'his warmest thanks'. Serjeant Sullivan, however, would not hear of this line of defence. Finally, he and Gavan Duffy persuaded Casement to plead Not Guilty. Sullivan intended to run the case on the grounds that the statute under which Casement was indicted (one of Edward III) did not relate to the evidence before the court. The statute provided that it was Treason 'If a man be adherent to the King's enemy in his Realm.' Sullivan's point on which he put great stock was that Casement's activity had been *outside* the realm.

A further advantage of pleading not guilty, Sullivan argued, would be that Casement would not have to give evidence and would therefore avoid a brutal and perhaps damaging cross examination by the Attorney-General. Casement was persuaded against his better judgment that the court would exercise a judicial attitude in estimating a point of law. When the trial opened at the Old Bailey on June 26, 1916, a plea was entered for the prisoner of Not Guilty.

The Lord Chief Justice, Rufus Isaacs, presided at the trial. The other judges were Avory and Horridge. The case was prosecuted by the Attorney-General. A less brazen advocate than F. E. Smith (by then Sir Frederick Smith) might have baulked at taking a case where the prisoner was charged with conspiring with the enemies of the Crown to commit Treason. This was precisely what Smith had done himself when he acted as Carson's galloper in 1912. Being the lawyer that he was, he must have been aware that he had been lucky to escape prosecution for his questionable activities then. Now, armoured by the dignity of his Office, he does not seem to have been in the least deterred by the past when he opened the prosecution's case against Casement. It was a bitter and unprofessional address, clearly in breach of the legal convention that a prosecutor should not seek to inflame the jury's mind by using an emotional approach. Most improperly the night before, Smith had sent off a copy of his opening speech to the American press, though he was aware that it contained matters which he knew he would not be able to present in evidence.

The prosecution called witnesses to show that Casement had attempted to enlist the aid of Irish prisoners of war serving in the British Army. Some of the witnesses were actually members of Casement's Brigade. Evidence was given of his arrest in Kerry and of his connection with the revolutionary movement in Ireland.

Sullivan then made legal submissions to the presiding judge submitting that there was not sufficient evidence to allow the case to go to the jury. These were rejected. Casement made a brief unsworn speech in the dock and Sullivan opened his client's case to the jury.

Sullivan shared one political belief with Casement, that it was the arming of the Ulster Volunteers and the encouragement given to them by the Conservative Party, that had precipitated the Rebellion in Ireland. As he unfolded his argument it became obvious that this was the central theme. What he hadn't reckoned with, however, was that one of the chief protagonists of these 'treasonable activities' was sitting on the same bench with them in the person of the Attorney-General, who heckled and bullied Sullivan, frequently rising to his feet and complaining to the Judge. This continued to the extent that Sullivan finally broke down and had to leave the Court without completing his address to the jury.

When the jury retired they were out for less than an hour before they reached their verdict of guilty. Roger Casement then spoke from the dock, giving his reasons why sentence should not be passed on him. It was the traditional stance of the Irish patriot. Speeches from the dock were part of Irish patriotic literature, and Casement meant to see that he would be included in it.

The theme of his address was that the exploitation of Ulster by the Conservatives had left patriotic Irishmen with no alternative but to seek to remedy the country's predicament by other means than constitutional ones.

'The Government had permitted the Ulster Volunteers to be armed by Englishmen, to threaten not merely an English Party in its hold on office, but to threaten that Party through the lives and blood of Irishmen. The battle was to be fought in Ireland in order that the political "outs" of today should be the "ins" of tomorrow in Great Britain.

'We had seen the working of the Irish constitution in the refusal of the Army of occupation at the Curragh to obey the orders of the Crown. And now that we were told that the first duty of an Irishman was to enter that army in return for a promissory note, payable after death, a scrap of paper that might or might not be redeemed, I felt over there in America that my first duty was to keep Irishmen at home for the only army that could safeguard our national existence.'

Casement looked significantly at the Attorney-General before he made his next remark. 'The difference between us was that the Unionist champions chose a path they felt would lead to the Woolsack; while I went on a road I knew must lead to the dock. And the event proves we were both right.' (Casement's prediction

108

did prove correct for in 1919, Sir Frederick Smith became Lord Chancellor and sat on the Woolsack.)

He indicated what he thought was the root of the bad relations between Great Britain and Ireland, the Imperial link. 'An Empire that can only be held together by one section of its governing population perpetually holding down and sowing dissension among a smaller but none the less governing section, must have some canker at its heart, some ruin at its root.' 'Conquest, my Lord,' he continued, 'gives no title, and if it exists over the body, it fails over the mind. It can exert no empire over men's reason and judgment and affections; and it is from this law of conquest without title to the reason, judgment, and affection of my own countrymen that I appeal.'

He ended with a simple claim that he had done what he had done as an Irishman. 'I did not land in England; I landed in Ireland. It was to Ireland I came; and to Ireland I wanted to come; and the last place I desired to land in was England. But for the Attorney-General of England there is only "England" – there is no Ireland, there is only the law of England – no right of Ireland; the liberty of Ireland and of Irishmen is to be judged by the power of England. Yet for me, the Irish outlaw, there is a land of Ireland, a right of Ireland, and a charter for all Irishmen to appeal to, in the last resort, a charter that even the very statutes of England cannot deprive us of – nay, more, a charter that Englishmen themselves assert as the fundamental bond of law that connects the two kingdoms.' Later, another fighter for freedom, Pandit Nehru, the Indian leader, was to relate how much this speech moved him and inspired him to work for the freedom of his own country.

Casement appealed his conviction in the House of Lords but predictably the appeal was rejected. His execution was fixed for August 3. A campaign for his reprieve was immediately begun in the United States and Britain. One difficulty in the United States was that President Wilson was, in the words of the British Ambassador to Washington at that time, 'by descent an Orangeman and Presbyterian'. He was not sympathetic and effectively quenched the efforts of congressmen to have Casement's case debated in the House of Representatives.

Conan Doyle and Bernard Shaw were among those who lent

their support to the campaign for Casement's reprieve in Britain. In America, William Randolph Hearst put the power of his chain of newspapers behind the Casement appeal. From South America, countries where Casement's humanitarian efforts were remembered, sent telegrams of protest to the British Cabinet.

An accusation that particularly revolted Casement was that he had shown himself ungrateful to the British Government by accepting a pension from them, and then going to Germany during the war. He was pleased when Shaw, with Irish wit, managed to put the matter in perspective for the Saxon.

Public opinion [Shaw wrote to the *Manchester Guardian*] seems to be influenced to some extent by the notion that because Casement received money for his work from the British Empire, and earned it with such distinction that he became personally famous and was knighted for it, and expressed himself as gentlemen do on such occasions, he is in the odious position of having bitten the hand that fed him. To the people who take this view I put my own case. I have been employed by Germany as a playwright for many years, and by the Austrian Emperor in the great theatre in Vienna which is part of his household. I have received thousands of pounds for my services. I was recognized in this way when the English theatres were contemptuously closed to me. I was compelled to produce my last important play (*Pygmalion*) in Berlin in order that it might not be prejudiced by the carefully telegraphed abuse of the English press. Am I to understand that it is therefore my duty to fight for Germany and Austria, and that, in taking advantage of the international reputation which I unquestionably owe to Germany more than to any other country to make the first statement of the case against her which could have convinced anybody outside England, I was biting the hand of the venerable Franz Josef, whose bread I had eaten? I cannot admit it for a moment. I hope I have not been ungrateful. I have refused to join in the popular game of throwing mud at the Germans, and I have said nothing against them that I did not say when many of our most ardent patriots were lighting illuminations and raising triumphal arches to welcome the Kaiser in London.

On August 2, the Cabinet finally rejected requests for reprieve and Casement was hanged on August 3. A significant factor about Casement's career is that though an Irish nationalist, he had until quite late in life supported the idea of a free Ireland within the British Empire. Indeed in 1900 when he was in South Africa, he strongly disapproved of the recruiting of Irishmen to fight for the Boers against the British Army. However, as he became immersed in the dealings of the Foreign Office, he began to conclude that when it came to dealing with colonial dependencies of which Ireland was one, the rules so ardently supported by democrats in Parliament were no proof against the activities of those who, at the end of all, had shown themselves to be in control of the sources of power.

A letter he wrote to a warder who had been kind to him while in prison showed that he had no hatred of England. 'You showed the best side of an Englishman's character – his native good heart. Whatever you think of my attitude towards your Government and the Realm, I would ask you to keep only one thing in that good heart of yours – and that is that a man might fight a country and its policy, and yet not hate an individual of that country.'

Those English who supported his reprieve came largely from the ranks of anti-imperialists, Fabians, Socialists, Pacifists. They shared the belief with Casement that the time had passed when a power such as that possessed by the British Empire should be concentrated in the hands of an elite. They had opposed his sentence on humanitarian grounds but in temperament they were light years away from him; Casement was a romantic whose dream was for a small country which held little interest for his well-intentioned English friends. How could they understand that when he landed from the German submarine after a ghastly journey and with the expectation that he was facing almost certain execution, his only thoughts were that he was back in his native land?

'The sandhills were full of skylarks rising in the dawn, the first I had heard for years – the first sound I heard through the surf was their song, as I waded through the breakers, and they kept rising all the time up to the old rath at Currsahone, where I stayed and sent the others on, and all round were primroses and wild violets and the singing of the skylarks in the air, and I was back in Ireland again.'

During Casement's trial, F. E. Smith produced to Serjeant Sullivan what he alleged were Casement's diaries. This was in an effort to secure from Casement's Counsel a plea of guilty but insane. The diaries contained details of a number of homosexual acts. The suggestion was not taken up by Sullivan. The diaries were afterwards circulated in influential circles in the United States to blacken Casement's character and to lessen sympathy for him so as to militate against his reprieve. It was a barbarous stratagem, understood perhaps if seen against the perilous situation in which Britain found herself at that time.

It has not been clearly established that the diaries are genuine throughout. There is, however, evidence to show that Casement may have had homosexual tastes. Recognizing this, British Intelligence lost no time in presenting him to the world as a monster with the traditional skill which had made them past masters of the art of converting a half truth into distortions of reality.

Chapter Twenty

Shortly after the Rising the tide began to turn. The country as a whole had been against the Rebellion. But the executions had shocked many. They showed the extent to which the rulers of the country were prepared to go.

At Christmas 1916 the first prisoners were let home from Frongoch Internment Camp in Wales. Their home-coming was uneventful, though there was considerably less hostility towards them than when they had left the country nine months before. By the time the third batch of prisoners was released in June, the situation had changed. Two seats had become vacant at Westminster through the death of sitting Members – Roscommon and South Longford. Sinn Fein decided to contest both seats. The Roscommon seat was won by Count Plunkett, father of the executed leader. Joseph McGuinness who was elected for South Longford was actually in jail when he received news of his victory. His election slogan had been 'Put him in to get him out.' Neither Plunkett nor McGuinness proposed to take their seat at Westminster. This was the first opportunity Sinn Fein had had to put Arthur Griffith's abstentionist policy into operation.

When the last batch of released prisoners landed at Kingstown Pier in June 1917, Eamon de Valera was first down the gangway. As the last surviving Commandant of the Rising he had a stirring reception. His long El Grecoesque face, with his wan smile of victory, singled him out from the other released men as they were brought in lorries through the cheering crowds en route to the city, and would become a symbol for many who saw in him then the man who would carry on the spirit of the leaders of the Rising.

Already de Valera was spoken of with reverence in many circles. His charisma was to be put to the test fairly soon. He had been chosen to contest the East Clare By-Election against Patrick Lynch, K.C., a member of John Redmond's Parliamentary Party. A month after his return, de Valera was elected M.P.

for East Clare by a large majority. *The Daily Express* said the following day that 'Sinn Fein has swept the country like a tidal wave and blotted out the Irish Party completely'.

A former Staff Captain in the Rising and A.D.C. to James Connolly had been amongst the first batch of prisoners released at Christmas. His name was Michael Collins. He was to become a major figure in the confrontation with the British during the next four years. Immediately he arrived home, Collins started to reorganize the Volunteers. His special concern was to build up the Irish Republican Brotherhood by selecting able, ruthless men who would form themselves into a Corps Elite.

Collins had had reservations about the Rising and regarded it as badly organized. Walking down the Dublin Quays after the Rising he had replied to a companion who said, 'Well it was a good fight, Mick' with, 'What do you mean a good fight . . . we lost didn't we.'

Thomas Ashe, a member of the Inner Circle and president of the I.R.B., had been arrested in August for a 'speech calculated to cause disaffection'. He had been condemned to death for his part in 1916 but had had his sentence commuted. On Thursday, September 20, 1917, Ashe went on hunger strike in protest against his imprisonment. Four days later after being forcibly fed, he died at 3 a.m. in the Mater Hospital.

Collins, along with Richard Mulcahy of the I.R.B., decided to organize a massive demonstration around Ashe's funeral. The body was laid out in Volunteer uniform in the Dublin City Hall. Armed Volunteers stood guard over it. On the day of the funeral, 9,000 Volunteers assembled to escort the coffin through the streets. 'The Black Raven' Pipe Band in kilts marched in front of the cortège. On each side of the hearse uniformed Volunteers marched with rifles and behind was an officer with a drawn sword. Countess Markievicz swung along out in front with her revolver in her belt.

Down by the Dublin Quays the cortège went. Then up through O'Connell Street through dense crowds to Glasnevin Cemetery. At the graveside Fianna Boy Scouts sounded the Last Post. Then the firing party fired volleys into the air. There was no oration at the graveside. After the volley, Michael Collins stepped out of the crowd in his officer's uniform. 'Nothing additional remains to be said,' he said. 'That volley which we have just heard is the only speech which it is proper to make above the grave of a dead Fenian.'

Ashe's death and funeral were a vital point in the resurgence of Sinn Fein. Coming on the heels of the successes at the Polls, this grim event helped to underline the necessity for some sort of alliance between the political programme of Sinn Fein and the physical force movement.

It also unleashed a flood of emotion over the country in some ways similar to that in 1916. Ashe's close friend, Sean O'Casey (the playwright), wrote a ballad, *The Lament for Thomas Ashe*, which was soon sung at gatherings throughout the country.

Ashe himself though more soldier than poet had written a hymn in prison which seemed to embody the essence of the sacrifice he would make some months later. This hymn, which after his death was inserted in many prayer books, though it was not of the calibre of the verse of the executed leaders, contributed to the swing of sympathy which was moving inexorably in the direction of Sinn Fein.

Let me carry your Cross for Ireland, Lord!
   The hour of her trial drawn near,
And the pangs and the pains of the sacrifice
   May be borne by comrades dear,
But, Lord, take me from the offering throng,
   There are many far less prepared,
Though anxious and all as they are to die
   That Ireland may be spared.

Let me carry your Cross for Ireland, Lord!
   My cares in this world are few,
And few are the tears will fall for me,
   When I go on my way to You.
Spare, oh! spare to their loved ones dear
   The brother and son and sire,
That the cause we love may never die
   In the land of our heart's desire.

Let me carry your Cross for Ireland, Lord!
　For Ireland weak with tears,
For the aged man of the clouded brow,
　And the child of the tender years;
For the empty homes of her golden plains;
　For the hopes of her future, too!
Let me carry your Cross for Ireland, Lord,
　For the cause of Roisin Dubh.[1]

[1] Ireland was often personified by poets through the name of a woman, Dark Rosaleen or Roisin Dubh.

Chapter Twenty-One

Tom Kettle once wrote 'Dublin Castle, if it did not know what the Irish people want, could not so infallibly have maintained its tradition of giving them the opposite.' A friend of Desmond Ryan, who fought in the Post Office in 1916, made a similar remark to him when they were sitting in the Café Cairo one day in the autumn of 1918. 'We have one great hope. That Ally has never failed us yet – the British Government. When our tank runs short of petrol, the British Government will tank us up all right.'

In 1918, though the trend towards Sinn Fein was impressive, there was no indication of any serious threat to the Irish Parliamentary Party. John Redmond still seemed to have the allegiance of the majority of people in the country. After all, hundreds of thousands of Southern Irishmen were out fighting for Britain and it was expected that once the war was over, Redmond would be in a position to reactivate the Home Rule Bill, already on the Statute Books.

In April 1918, the British Government embarked on a policy which, if it had been devised by their closest supporters, couldn't have helped Sinn Fein more. Pressured by Sir Henry Wilson, the Chief of the Imperial General Staff, and with the War effort tottering in France as a result of the Ludendorff push, Lloyd George agreed to a Conscription Bill for Ireland. This meant that all able-bodied Irishmen would be liable for the call-up.

Nothing could have been more calculated to create a united National front in Ireland. John Redmond's Irish Party and Sinn Fein appeared on the same platforms in protest against the Bill. The Irish Catholic Hierarchy opposed the Bill vehemently and issued a statement in which they said, 'It is lawful to resist Conscription by force'. This was a vital concession for Sinn Fein. It meant that the principle of resistance by force to certain British measures had been established. It would not be difficult later on to extend the analogy.

The British General Election took place in December 1918, just after the end of the Great War. It resulted in the virtual annihilation of Redmond's Home Rule Party, which had dominated the political scene in Ireland for twenty years. Sinn Fein swept the decks with 73 seats. The Irish Party won only six.

This result was to have the effect of finally discrediting agitation by constitutional means in the Irish struggle for self-government.

A. J. P. Taylor, in *English History 1914–45* has described the decision to enforce conscription as 'the decisive moment at which Ireland ceded from the union'.

In a letter to a member of the Cabinet, Lord Haldane, written in October 1918, W. B. Yeats anticipates in prescient fashion the effect the threat of conscription would have on the mood of the country:

Dear Lord Haldane,

I have just returned to Dublin from the West of Ireland, where I have been living for months. I am alarmed at the state of feeling here and there. I write to you because you are a man of letters, and we, therefore, may speak the same language. I have no part in politics and no liking for politics, but there are moments when one cannot keep out of them. I have met nobody in close contact with the people who believes that conscription can be imposed without the killing of men, and perhaps of women. Lady Gregory, who knows the country as few know it, and has taken down, for instance, hundreds of thousands of words in collecting folk-lore from cottage to cottage and has still many ways of learning what is thought about it – is convinced that the women and children will stand in front of their men and receive the bullets. I do not say that this will happen, but I do say that there is in this country an extravagance of emotion which few Englishmen, accustomed to more objective habits of thought, can understand. There is something oriental in the people, and it is impossible to say how great a tragedy may lie before us. The British Government, it seems to me, is rushing into this business in a strangely trivial frame of mind. I hear of all manner of opinions being taken except the opinion of those who have some knowledge of the popular psychology. I hear even of weight being given to the opinions of clergymen of the Church of Ireland, who, as a class, are more isolated from their neighbours than any class anywhere known to me. I find in people here in Dublin a sense of strain and expectancy which makes even strangers speak something of their mind. I was ordering some coal yesterday, and I said: 'I shall be in such and such a house for the next four months.' The man at the counter, a stranger to me, muttered: 'Who, in Ireland, can say where he will be in four months?' Another man, almost a stranger, used nearly those very words speaking to me some two weeks ago. There is a danger of a popular hysteria that may go to any height or any whither. There is a return to that sense of crisis which followed the Rising. Some two months after the Rising I called on a well-known Dublin doctor, and as I entered his room, an old cabinet-maker went out. The doctor said to me: 'That man has just said a very strange thing. He says there will be more trouble yet, for "The young men are mad jealous of their leaders for being shot".' That jealousy is still in the country. It is not a question as to whether it is justified or not justified for those men believe – an incredible thought, perhaps, to Englishmen – that the Childers Committee reported truthfully as to the overtaxation of Ireland, that the population of Ireland has gone down one-half through English mis-government, that the union of Ireland, in our time, was made impossible because England armed the minority of people with rifles and machine-guns. When they think to themselves: 'Now England expects us to die for her', is it wonderful that they say to themselves afterwards: 'We shall bring our deaths to a different market'. I read in the newspaper yesterday that over three hundred thousand Americans have landed in France in a month, and it seems to me a strangely wanton thing that England, for the sake of fifty thousand Irish soldiers, is prepared to hollow another trench between the countries and fill it with blood. If that is done England will only suffer in reputation, but Ireland will suffer in her character, and all the work of my lifetime and that of my fellow-workers, all our efforts to clarify and sweeten the popular mind, will be destroyed and Ireland, for another hundred years, will live in the sterility of her bitterness.

Yours sincerely,
W. B. YEATS

The Irish Party at Westminster was finished. In March 1918, John Redmond died a broken man, his life's work in ruins.

The central point in the Sinn Fein policy in the General Election of 1918 had been abstention from Westminster by elected representation, the same policy first put forward by Arthur Griffith in 1905.

Candidates would use the election machinery provided by the British in Ireland, but once returned would refuse to take their seats at Westminster and instead, set up a rival Parliament in Dublin, which would administer the affairs of the country in defiance of Britain.

When the Abstentionist Parliament (named the Dail) had its first meeting in the Mansion House, Dublin, on January 21, 1919, the majority of the Members were in British jails. They had been arrested under various pretexts in the previous six months. When the roll was called, the reply 'Faoi Glas ag Gallaibh' (imprisoned by the foreigner), was given thirty-six times. Only thirty-seven elected representatives were present. The Declaration of Independence was read and passed by those in attendance.

'Whereas the Irish people is by right a free people:

'And whereas for seven hundred years the Irish people had never ceased to repudiate and has repeatedly protested in arms against foreign usurpation:

'And whereas the Irish Republic was proclaimed in Dublin has been, based upon force and fraud and maintained by military occupation against the declared will of the people:

'And whereas the Irish Republic was proclaimed in Dublin on Easter Monday, 1916, by the Irish Republican Army, acting on behalf of the Irish people:

'We solemnly declare foreign government in Ireland to be an invasion of our national right which we will never tolerate, and we demand the evacuation of our country by the English Garrison:

'We claim for our national independence the recognition and support of every free nation in the world, and we proclaim that independence to be a condition precedent to international peace hereafter.'

The important part of the declaration was the demand that the British should leave. The Abstentionist Parliament was irrevocably linked by it to the principles contained in the 1916 Proclamation.

Three delegates to the Peace Conference in Paris were appointed – Arthur Griffith, Eamon de Valera[1] and Count Plunkett. After some other motions had been proposed and accepted, the meeting concluded.

It is important to examine Griffith's position in relation to the physical force movement at this stage. His policy was still essentially one of passive resistance. For this reason he had not taken part in the Rising. But Griffith had the confidence of the physical force movement. They recognized him as the political philosopher of the separatist tradition.

Richard Mulcahy, Chief of Staff of the I.R.A. during the Anglo-Irish war, has told the author that in his opinion it was Griffith's 'United Irishman' that had kept the flame of separatism alive during the great Home Rule agitation in the first decade of the century. After the Rising Griffith recognized that a means would have to be found of fusing the Sinn Fein political policy with the popular feeling that had swung over to the Volunteers as a result of the executions. He was continually on the look out for an Avatar who would bring both parties together. In de Valera Griffith believed he had found this person. The East Clare election had shown that de Valera's personality exercised an almost mystical effect on the people. He had the glamour of being the last surviving Commandant of the Rising and a Spanish name. As well he had begun to show a remarkable flair for

[1] De Valera had been arrested the previous May and imprisoned in Lincoln Jail.

politics which, combined with his revolutionary background, drew Griffith towards him.

At the 1917 National Convention of Sinn Fein Griffith stood down in favour of de Valera who was then elected. Griffith's speech at the Ard Fheis in April that year shows the reverence he had for the young soldier-politician.

'De Valera is a man in whose judgments and rectitude we can absolutely trust. A great leader, a man with a wonderful judgment such as I have never met in a young man except in Parnell.

'Since Parnell's day there was not a man to equal de Valera and I am sure in following him and standing by him loyally we shall bring the Irish cause to the goal for which many Irishmen in hopeful generations suffered and we have lived in hopeful generations.'

On April 1, at an extraordinary session of the Dail, de Valera was elected President. In pursuit of Griffith's Sinn Fein policy a Cabinet was formed which included Griffith himself as Minister for Home Affairs, Cathal Brugha for Defence, Collins for Finance, Cosgrave for Local Government, Barton for Agriculture, Eoin MacNeill for Industry, Count Plunkett for Foreign Affairs, Countess Markievicz for Labour and Richard Mulcahy as Minister for Defence.

The Cabinet covered a wide spectrum of the social scale. Two of the new Ministers – Robert Barton and Countess Markievicz – were of the landed gentry class. Barton had been a Lieutenant in the British Army during the 1916 Rising. He had been so impressed by the demeanour of the prisoners in his charge that he later joined the Volunteers himself, rising to the rank of Commandant. He had been arrested for seditious speech sometime before the Dail met in January but Collins had conveniently arranged his escape to coincide with the Extraordinary General Meeting in April.

On the surface the formation of a Dail Cabinet appeared a somewhat Utopian procedure. But when put into operation, the Sinn Fein policy was to have striking success. The Department of Finance, under Michael Collins, floated a National Loan which would raise over a million pounds. Republican Courts of Justice and Equity would be set up. These operated in twenty-three out of the thirty-two counties. In the end, the British administration was to become paralysed as the majority of people in the country simply ignored existing institutions.

These policies escalated until Britain found herself resorting to measures which were to damage her prestige in the eyes of the world.

As British military policy became more and more frightful, Republican resistance grew. This time, however, they were not taking up arms as an unpopular minority group but as the official army of the elected Government of the people. The real importance of the Sinn Fein philosophy is that it provided a formula by which Collins' guerilla force, the first one of its kind in modern times, could derive its authority from an elected Parliament.

Later, when the Anglo-Irish war had finished, it was probably the fact that the rebel army derived its moral authority from the Dail which made possible the transition from revolution to peace, and the setting up of institutions which would prove durable in the ensuing decades, when subjected to armed threats from right and left.

After the first Dail meeting had been concluded, Collins decided to organize de Valera's escape from Lincoln Jail in England.

One of de Valera's fellow prisoners, Sean Milroy, sent out a postcard on which a cartoon was drawn. The cartoon depicted a man with a key. A key similar to the one drawn on the postcard was made. Then Collins went over in February with Harry Boland to personally supervise the escape.

The rescuers went up to a gate at the side of the prison and pushed the key in the lock. Unfortunately it broke as they tried to turn it. De Valera, waiting anxiously inside, in a fury pushed a key made inside the jail into the lock and by an extraordinary stroke of luck, shoved the broken one out.

Collins and Boland quickly hurried him away to where a car was waiting.

De Valera spent nearly two months in the vicinity of Manchester before he returned to Ireland in March.

Chapter Twenty-Two

As had been anticipated, the British policy of oppression swung into action soon after the Dail had met in January 1919. In the six months following, 18,215 arrests were made. In September the Dail was declared illegal. Cabinet Ministers had to go on the run and conduct their business from secret offices in the city. Political commentators went so far as to conjecture that the Government was deliberately trying to invite rebellion. The composition of the British Cabinet Committee formed to draw up a new scheme for Ireland was not calculated to assuage Nationalist fears. Walter Long, a notorious 'Ulster rebel' in 1912, was Chairman of the Committee and it included others who had conspired against the Crown in Ulster before the war.

'The general staff of Carson at the time of the Ulster revolt who had since made their way to place and power' is how Silvain Briolly, a French journalist living in Dublin, summed up the Government's Irish Committee.

On November 30,1919, *The Times* said:

There are strong proofs that there exists a powerful conspiracy against the prospect of peace in Ireland ... The progress which the Committee on Home Rule are said to have made towards a frank solution of the Irish problem is doubtless far from welcome to those elements which in Ireland regard any departure from the status quo as a menace to their privileges and interests. It would suit the plans of the obstructionists much better if Sinn Fein Ireland were itself to wreck the project. It is difficult to believe that the repressive measures so tardily taken are not the deliberate development of an intrigue ... We fear that the Executive in Ireland has acted, with or without the complicity of members of the Cabinet, to arouse in Ireland such a state of feeling, if not of rebellion, that a settlement may become impossible.

The policy of oppression had played right into Michael Collins' hands. An inspired revolutionary, he recognized that the time had come to put his ideas to the test. In addition to his position as Minister for Finance in the Dail, he had also been appointed Director of Intelligence in the Ministry of Defence. Since 1917, Collins had been working to reorganize the I.R.B. Now he intended to use the fruits of his labour.

Collins was a man of many gifts, but his outstanding quality was his ability to penetrate to the heart of a complex problem in a second or two. It was he who first isolated the formula which subsequent guerilla organizations throughout the world were to use against colonialism. He concluded from his study of previous rebellions that they had failed because the authorities had obtained information in advance of what was to take place. They obtained this from informers, and through the system of para-military police established throughout the country.

Unlike their counterparts in Britain, the Royal Irish Constabulary were an armed force, and resembled more a military organization than the English concept of what a police force should be.

Collins was the first to recognize that without these able adjuncts to government, it would be impossible to organize an adequate resistance to a well conducted guerilla campaign.

In a phrase, he intended to 'Put out the eyes of the British' and make their position in the country impossible. Later he explained his policy in an interview with the New York journal *American*.

'England could always reinforce her army', he wrote. 'She could replace every soldier that she lost. But there were others indispensable for her purposes who were not so easily replaced. To paralyze the British machine it was necessary to strike at individuals. Without her spies England was helpless. It was only by means of their accumulated knowledge that the British machine could operate. Without their police throughout the country, how could they find the man they wanted? Without their criminal agents in the capital how could they carry out that "removal" of the leaders that they considered essential for their victory?

'The most potent of these spies were Irishmen enlisted in the British service, and drawn from the small farmer and labourer class.

125

'We struck at individuals, and by doing so we cut their lines of communication, and we shook their morale. And we conducted the conflict, difficult as it was, with the unequal terms imposed by the enemy, as far as possible, according to the rules of war.'

Before he put out their 'eyes', Collins proposed to find out how much the British knew about his plans. If the informer had hitherto been the curse of Irish freedom fights, Collins now proposed to use this traditional Irish product against their employers. Early on he found an excellent contact in the heart of the Administration at Dublin Castle. This was Eamonn Broy, of the G Division of the Dublin Metropolitan Police.

'For a long time', Broy told the author, 'I had been on the lookout for someone to whom I could entrust information that would be useful in a national struggle. Then one day I got to see Collins. Immediately I met him, I knew he was the man who could beat the British and I decided to work for him from then on.'

Broy was soon to find out what working for Collins meant. One day, Collins blandly asked him to bring him into Police Headquarters in Dublin at night so that he could go through the files there.

Much against his better judgment, Broy managed to arrange to slip Collins into the Police Offices in Brunswick Street, where the intelligence files were kept, after 11 p.m. at night. He and Collins remained there until 7 o'clock the next morning. Broy was understandably nervous while Collins worked his way methodically through the files as if he were a police employee. When he came across his own file he just gave a grunt and put it in his briefcase. Broy breathed a sigh of relief as they got out on the street early the following morning. Then to his horror Collins insisted on going back. He had left some documents behind and refused to go away without them. The whole enterprise concluded smoothly as Collins on his way out with a debonair look, strode past the policeman at the door with a blithe 'Good morning'.

Once he had this information, Collins began to construct his own intelligence system. He had a pigeon-hole mind and could carry a vast amount of information in his head at one time. Often he could leap from fact to fact in an instant, relating the most unlikely pieces of information to one another and arriving at a conclusion which enabled him to place responsibility on a particular person. His gifts for detection were astonishing. With a reliable flow of information coming in to him from other detectives (besides Broy) whom he had induced to work for him, he began to build up a formidable counter-espionage system.

A pattern began to emerge from the information brought to him. It seemed that there were three particular policemen, all members of the G Division, who were key figures in arranging the arrest of Republicans.

As soon as he had definitely pin-pointed his men, Collins decided that they were to be done away with.

Collins was to be criticized subsequently for the ruthless methods he employed.

His answer to that would have been that his methods worked.

Later he used to say: 'We applied the pressure in the proper places. World opinion has forced the British to take the step of having these conferences with us. They want to clear their name with the World.'

The first killing authorized by Collins took place on July 31, 1919, when Detective Smyth of the Dublin Metropolitan Police, a well-known Republican hater, was shot outside his home.

The author asked one of the men who had given the order for the killing whether it was possible to justify the shooting down of a fellow Irishman almost in front of his wife and family.

' "Dog" Smyth had been warned on a number of occasions to lay off Republicans or he would be shot,' was the answer I got. 'He persisted and met the fate he asked for.'

Collins intended to make sure that the Dublin Castle police would be left under no illusion that the Smyth killing was an isolated act. On September 12, Detective Daniel Hoey was shot dead outside police headquarters in Dublin. On December 1, Detective Barton was shot in the street and died later.

The authorities were now thoroughly alarmed. They were losing key men in their spy system. What's more, they realized that Collins knew who the key men were and was determined to eliminate them.

In an effort to halt the killings, Detective Inspector F. Redmond was brought down from Belfast in December after

Barton's death. Redmond was an alert police officer who came to Dublin where he was given the rank of Assistant Commissioner.

He must have worked efficiently or else had a great deal of luck during the first few weeks in Dublin because by January he was able to announce to a fellow detective that he had arranged a meeting with Collins. The detective, who happened to be Dave Neligan, one of Collins' men, immediately sent a message to the Big Fellow through Eamonn Broy.

'I ran like hell', Broy has told the author, 'and just managed to reach Collins in time. He was to meet the Castle informer in less than an hour. I blurted out my information between gasps. Collins sat there quite still looking at me. He remained silent for a minute or two. Then suddenly instructions began to pour out of his mouth. In a minute or two the plans for the meeting had been changed and the danger averted.

'I shall never forget seeing the way Collins' mind worked. It was like putting information into a computer.'

A few days later Collins' men killed Redmond as he was on his way to the Standard Hotel in Harcourt Street, where he had rooms. (The killing was carefully planned. Paddy Daly and another man had stayed in the hotel two weeks beforehand to plot out Redmond's movements.)

'We knew he had a bulllet-proof waistcoat on', Joe Dolan, one of the Volunteers who took part in the killing, told me, 'so we shot him in the head. He didn't come up to Standard.' As he said this, Dolan blurted out an almost schoolboy giggle.

Collins now had a group around him of ruthless guerilla fighters. It was not the least of his gifts that he knew how to select efficient operators.

In a country paralysed by centuries of oppression it was not easy to find men with the ruthlessness and discipline necessary to carry out Collins' orders. But, as Chairman of the I.R.B., he had come in contact with the cream of the revolutionary movement and it was from them that he selected his first teams. He had created an Intelligence Section attached to General Headquarters staff, which was run by Frank Thornton, Liam Tobin and Tom Cullen. They correlated and shredded the vast amount of material and information that came in from Collins' different sources.

He would obtain information from a wide variety of people. For instance, he had constructed a network of people among the railway men, who carried messages to him from the country and back again from him to the different brigades. Another group worked in the Post Office intercepting letters. On the Liverpool B. + I. Boat his contact was Neil Kerr, the Purser, who, as well, brought over reports from Collins' friend Sam Maguire who worked in the Civil Service in London. Collins had a knack of picking up miscellaneous sources of information which he could use to complete the mosaic. The billiard marker for instance in the Kildare Street Club proved unusually useful in supplying information that slipped from the lips of landed gentlemen in between potting the balls into the pockets. It was the Canteen Manager in King George V Military Hospital, a man named Houlihan, who smuggled out the gun that was used in the killing of Commissioner Redmond.

It was typical of Collins that he would use a place as innocuous as a public library to coordinate his various sources of information. This was in Capel Street, about five minutes away from Dublin Castle. The librarian there, Thomas Gay, was an I.R.B. man who, through a Collins' contact in the Dublin Corporation, had arranged that all the porters and workers in the library were sympathetic to Sinn Fein. The library was half-way between Dublin Castle and Vaughan's Hotel, where Brigade Officers used to stay when they came up to see Collins. It was an ideal location to make contact. Collins always insisted that Gay would have a selection of books laid out for him. Arriving in his usual rush Collins would flick through the pages and if he didn't like them he would dip into the library shelves and get instead something he preferred.

Collins kept his Intelligence sources in different sections. One group might not know that another group was working for him. This occasionally led to ludicrous situations, such as the occasion when Tobin and Cullen spent an afternoon shadowing Broy and Neligan, the Dublin Castle detectives, who were actually on their way to Collins to bring him information and thought they were being followed by English spies.

The purpose behind this almost obsessive secrecy was that if one group were captured, even under torture they would not be in a position to impart information.

When Collins had decided, through his Intelligence system, that a man was a spy or that his continued activity was a danger to the movement, he gave orders to the 'squad' to execute him. The 'squad' were a select group of marksmen chosen specially by Collins as an execution group. They included Joe Dolan, Vincent Byrne, Joe Leonard, Charlie Dalton, Paddy Daly and Bill Stapleton. Because they were twelve in number, they were known as 'The Twelve Apostles'. Bill Stapleton has told the author of the method of working of the Squad.

> Tobin or Cullen would come down and tell us who we were to get. It might be one of the Igoe Gang or a British spy sent over to shoot Collins. Two or three of us would go out with an Intelligence Officer walking in front of us, maybe about ten or fifteen yards. His job was to identify the man we were to shoot. Often we would be walking the streets the whole day without meeting our man. It meant going without lunch. But other times the Intelligence staff would have their information dead on and we would see our quarry immediately we came to the place we had been told he would be at. The Intelligence Officer would then signal to us in the following way. He would take off his hat and greet the marked man. Of course, he didn't know him. As soon as he did this we would shoot. We had to accept the G.H.Q. knew the right men to shoot. We knew that very great care was taken that this was so. As a result we didn't feel we had to worry. We were, after all, only soldiers doing our duty. I often went in and said a little prayer for the people that we'd shot, afterwards.

In the beginning the Squad operated from the Antient Concert Room in Brunswick Street where James Joyce and John McCormack had once sung. But these premises proved cramped and unsuitable and, after pestering Collins for some time, the Squad were finally given premises in Abbey Street. They reconditioned this as a painter's and decorator's offices. Stapleton chose the name George Moreland because he says 'it sounded Protestant and Jewish'. Prospective clients would be greeted by one of the Squad in overalls when they went to give their custom. The order would be taken in great detail and when it was filled in the client would be told that since their orders were very heavy it would take six months to fulfil the present one. This usually sent the client hurrying somewhere else.

Their methods were not dissimilar from those of the Nodnaya Volya, the Russian Revolutionary Group which hired a cheese shop in Moscow in order to assassinate Alexander II in 1874, except that the Russian assassins had not taken the trouble to study the cheese trade, a fact which gave rise to suspicion among their customers, while the 'Squad' had one or two expert artisans among them who were able to convince prospective customers of the legitimacy of their trade.

As the Squad's premises in Abbey Street were only a few minutes' walk from Dublin Castle, it was not hard to nip out, engage in a gun battle with G men and be back in overalls a short time afterwards. One day Joe Dolan and another Squad man were sent up from Abbey Street in a taxi to get the porter of the Wicklow Hotel who, it had just been discovered, had betrayed a number of people to the British. Though the Wicklow was only five minutes' walk away, they hired a taxi. When they reached the hotel they asked the porter to take their bags. Thus burdened, they shot him.

Another day a message came down that one of Collins' G men in the Castle would come down Parliament Street with a Sergeant Roche – Roche had come to Dublin from Tipperary for the purpose of identifying Sean Treacy (the Vice-Brigadier of the Tipperary Brigade) who had been shot in Talbot Street the previous day. Paddy Daly and Bill Stapleton walked out of Abbey Street, across the river into Parliament Street where they saw Collins' spy with Sergeant Roche, chatting away as they walked along the street. The detective held his finger over Roche to identify him. Daly fired. The detective then calmly turned and went back to the Castle to report that he and his companion had been attacked by gunmen and that Roche was dead.

The Squad was drawn mostly from the clerk or artisan class. But it was not exclusively so. Charlie Dalton was from a well-off family on the north side of the city. His brother, Emmet (the Director of munitions on the I.R.A. G.H.Q. staff) had been a British officer in the war and won the M.C. at Ginchy. Emmet continued to play soccer for the fashionable Bohemians team right through the Black and Tan war, frequently playing matches against British Regiments behind the barbed wire which had been erected around the barracks precisely to keep men of his kind from entering for purposes other than sport.

Chapter Twenty-Three

While Collins was conducting his campaign in Dublin, the Volunteers had begun an initiative in the countryside.[1]

Volunteer Brigades were being organized in Cork, Limerick, Tipperary, Clare, Longford, Monaghan and Waterford. It was in these areas that the Volunteers were most active and were therefore able to organize up to brigade strength.

I.R.A. men shortly to become legends in the countryside were General Tom Barry of West Cork, Liam Lynch of North Cork, the Brennan Brothers from Clare, Sean McKeown of Longford, Sean Moylan of Waterford, Eoin O'Duffy of Monaghan.

Some of the officers like Tom Barry had been with the British Army. The training they had received during the Great War was invaluable in enabling them to instruct and train the Volunteers under their control.

There was no shortage of recruits. Young men rushed to join the I.R.A. They were mostly of good character, fit, teetotal and adventurous. Here was a chance at last to serve Ireland against the enemy.

The towns and villages they had come from were virtually feudal demesnes. On the outskirts of each town was the 'Big House' owned by the local Lord, whose title, of course, had been conferred by the English king.

The 'Big House' dispensed patronage to the numerous people in its employment – servants, gamekeepers, labourers, stewards. Shopkeepers in the towns deferred to the owner of the 'Big

[1] It is difficult to define accurately when the Irish Volunteers became the Irish Republican Army. Under the direction of I.R.B. men like Collins and Mulcahy the Volunteers had been reorganized throughout the country after the Rising. The Volunteer paper *An T-Oglach* (The Young Warrior) would say in December 1918 that 'the Irish Volunteers are the Army of the Irish Republic'. About this time the term Irish Republican Army came into use. The I.R.A. were distinct from the I.R.B. (Irish Republican Brotherhood), a secret organization, some of whose members were in the Volunteers and some of whom were not.

House' who was responsible for a good deal of their trade. They were also dependent on the goodwill of the Garrison Forces quartered in the town who took up a substantial portion of their custom. In the six Garrison towns of West Cork, Bandon, Clonakilty, Dunmanway, Skibbereen, Bantry and Castletown Bere, there were three thousand troops stationed.

On lands owned by the 'Big House' were many Protestant farmers. Usually, these could be relied on to support the activities of the Garrison. Throughout the countryside were pockets of Royalism, small gentry, retired naval and army officers and retired colonial officials.

The atmosphere of the Garrison towns was aggressively British. The State schools, where the children were educated up to fourteen years of age were designed to keep the pupil ignorant of Irish history and culture for they were not taught the Gaelic language. The poetry they learnt was by Englishmen – Keats, Tennyson, Wordsworth. The battles they had to memorize were Trafalgar, Agincourt, Waterloo. And the kings and queens whose reigns they were induced to commit to memory were exclusively English ones.

An assessment of the type of person who formed the nucleus of the I.R.A. in the countryside has come from a Lieutenant General in the British Army, Sir Henry Lawson.

The captains of volunteers appear to have been almost all quite young men, farmers' sons for the most part, some of them schoolmasters, most with what, for their class, must be considered a good deal of education, ignorant, however, of the world and of many things, but, as a class, transparently sincere and single-minded, idealists, highly religious for the most part, and often with an almost mystical sense of duty to their country. These men gave to the task of organizing their volunteers their best in mind and spirit. They fought against drunkenness and self-indulgence, and it is no exaggeration to say that, as a class, they represented all that was best in the countryside.

They and their volunteers were trained to discipline, they imbibed the military spirit, the sense of military honour, etc., and then, as now, they looked upon their army as one in a very real sense; an organization demanding implicit obedience and self-abnegation from rank to rank.

The Irish Republican Army seems to be particularly free from ruffians of the professional type, and the killings of police and others, sometimes under circumstances which evoke our horror, were almost certainly done by members of the I.R.A. acting under military orders – young men imbued with no personal feeling against their victims, with no crimes to their record, and probably then shedding blood for the first time in their lives . . .

Behind their organization there is the spirit of a nation – of a nation which is certainly not in favour of murder, but which, on the whole, sympathizes with them and believes that the members of the I.R.A. are fighting for the cause of the Irish people.

One of the advantages that the I.R.A. had as a guerilla force was that they were anonymous. Anonymity could only help them, of course, if they could rely on support from the civilian population. Once they were sure of shelter from the people, they had a decided advantage over the enemy, which would compensate for their lack of numbers and arms. In the end it became impossible for Crown Forces to segregate I.R.A. guerillas from the rest of the population without resorting to methods which, in themselves, proved self-defeating.

Another advantage the Volunteers had over the enemy was their knowledge of local terrain. After an engagement they could fade into the countryside, using hills, mountains and rivers which they had known since their boyhood, to cover their retreat. General Tom Barry has given an account of the training methods used by the Flying Columns under his command.

As the men arrived in camp, they were detailed to sections and section commanders appointed. Their first parade was to listen to a talk on the plan of defence and security measures to be enforced. The men were told to act as if they were expecting attack at any hour of the day or night, and most detailed instructions were issued. For the next hour they practised occupying their defence positions, aiming and trigger pressing and moving in extended order as directed. It was an unorthodox approach to training, but the circumstances necessitated the departure. After all, if an attack had come, all that really would have mattered, would have been that the men would obey orders, shoot straight and move in proper formation. Their ability to salute or to form fours smartly would not have been a consideration.

From eight in the morning until six in the evening the men drilled and trained. Close orders, extended order, arms drill and elementary tactics occupied the first four days. During the remaining three days more advanced movements were undertaken and special attention was given to 're-drilling'. In this each officer, in turn, took command of a section and handled it for an hour or so. Attack and defence exercises were a feature of the training, and after these, at a signal, all would come together to talk over and criticize the movements. Situations were envisaged of engaging the enemy at a stated strength, moving in a certain formation, and officers were appointed, in turn, to command the Column. The officers showed an extraordinary keenness on all parades but particularly for sham battles.

Many statements have been made by ministers and generals in various countries on the necessity for long periods of training before even an infantry soldier is ready for action. This is utter nonsense when applied to volunteers for guerilla warfare. After only one week of collective training, this Flying Column of intelligent and courageous fighters was fit to meet an equal number of soldiers from any regular army in the world, and hold its own battle, if not in barrackyard ceremonial.

The first Column attack in the South was by the Cork No. 2 Brigade, led by Commandant Liam Lynch, who was later to command the first Southern Division. He and his group ambushed a detachment of the King's Shropshire Light Infantry on their way to Church Service. As the soldiers marched in fours down the road, Lynch blew a blast on his whistle and called on them to surrender.

When they refused, the Volunteers opened fire and killed one soldier and wounded four. All Lynch's men made their escape, after relieving the ambushed soldiers of their arms and ammunition. Next day the Shropshires went berserk and looted and burnt the town of Fermoy, causing damage to the extent of over £3,000. This engagement took place in September 1919 and set the pattern for other I.R.A. attacks. Soon the ambush of troops and police became commonplace in the countryside.

As police lorries or armoured cars with troops in them ambled through the country roads, they would be called upon to surrender. Then a Column, concealed behind hedges and ditches, would open fire on them. Often mines were laid to explode under the first lorry. On other occasions the engagement began with the hurling of a grenade. This was followed by rifle fire from sections concealed along each side of the road.

This was a new form of warfare and it was understandable that the British refused to recognize it as such. It was common in military circles to refer to it as 'Ditch murder'. Later, Mao Tse Tung, Tito, General Giap, Che Guevara and General Grivas were to make it respectable. But now, though Ireland was officially in a state of war, Britain refused to grant captured I.R.A. men military status under the Hague and Geneva Conventions. From time to time I.R.A. prisoners were shot or hanged. This compelled the I.R.A. to take reprisals. Generally, however, they behaved with scrupulous fairness towards British prisoners whom they captured.

Brigadier-General Lucas of the Shropshire Regiment, who was taken by Lynch's men and held for a month before he escaped, had fishing and shooting facilities allowed him while he was a prisoner. After his escape he spoke of 'the very courteous and gentlemanly treatment' he had received.

For soldiers who behaved according to military convention, Brigade Commanders like Tom Barry had nothing but respect. 'For instance,' he told the author, 'Colonel Hudson of the King's Liverpools was a thorough gentleman who always treated our prisoners well. On one occasion we found some mess bills in a captured uniform and sent them back to Colonel Hudson for his officers. I asked him at the same time could he kindly return my only suit which had been captured by his men. This he very kindly did.

'On the other hand, you had a person like Major Percival with the Essex Regiment, who was a practising sadist. I can tell you

I wasn't very put out when later he made a coward of himself by surrendering to the Japanese when he was in command at Singapore.'

It was Barry who turned the Flying Column concept into what he termed 'the spearhead of the People's Army'. Certainly the victory of Barry's Brigade at Kilmichael and Crossbarry was to have a remarkable effect on the morale of guerilla fighters throughout the rest of Ireland.

On November 21, 1920, Barry's Brigade ambushed a detachment of Auxiliaries at Kilmichael on the road between Macroom and Dunmanway. After some very severe hand-to-hand fighting, eighteen of the British were killed while the Flying Column only suffered three losses. The army lorries were set on fire and the arms and equipment of the enemy were quickly stored away by the Volunteers.

The shock of victory and the spectacle of the dying and wounded unnerved some of the Column who hadn't been in battle before. With the practised eye of a professional soldier, Barry recognized this, and made his men form fours and go through arms and foot drill for five minutes to restore their morale. (It was the exception rather than the rule for members of this Flying Column to be older then twenty-one.)

The other major engagement at Crossbarry took place on March 19, 1921, when a determined effort was made by Crown Forces to eliminate Barry's Flying Column. Over a thousand troops drawn from the 1st Essex, 2nd Hampshires, the 1st Manchesters and the 120 Auxiliaries from Macroom Castle began a massive sweeping up operation under General Strickland and Brigadier-General Higginson.

Their aim was to destroy the Column completely. Barry as a result of the sweeping operation found himself under attack from three directions at once. Instead of retreating, he decided to take on the enemy full face, though he was out-numbered ten to one. At Crossbarry on the old main road to Cork City, he ambushed three detachments of soldiers and police. Twenty-nine British were killed and forty-seven wounded, while the I.R.A. lost only three.

Throughout the engagement a piper walked up and down playing Irish war tunes to encourage the men of the Column.

Ironically, Scottish Regiments and Irish Regiments going into battle in the British Army had always had a piper to lead them over the top. Now this old Gaelic custom had returned to the land of its origin. Barry, remembering the effect it had had on the men he had served with in the British Army, had enlisted a piper friend to lead the Column into action.

If there were any doubts that the I.R.A. was 'A People's Army' operating under the authority of Dail Eireann, de Valera dissolved these in a statement that he made to American news-agencies about the time of the Crossbarry attack.

'We took office knowing that the people wanted us to be a government in fact as well as in name . . .

'One of our first governmental acts was to take over control of the voluntary armed forces of the nation. From the Irish Volunteers we fashioned the Irish Republican Army to be the military arm of the Government. This army is, therefore, a reg-ular State force, under the control of elected representatives and under organization and a discipline imposed by those representa-tives, and under officers who hold their commissions under a warrant from these representatives. The Government is, there-fore, responsible for the actions of this army. These actions are not the acts of irresponsible individuals or groups, therefore, nor is the I.R.A. as the enemy would have one believe, a praetorian guard. It is the national army of defence.'

On Easter Sunday 1920, a hundred Inland Revenue buildings and 350 deserted R.I.C. Barracks were burned by the I.R.A. Large numbers of police stationed in the outlying districts had been driven into the towns. The burning of the empty barracks was a symbolic gesture which emphasized the growing impotency of the force.

Resignations about this time were wide-spread. As a result of I.R.A. success certain police officers began to encourage desper-ate measures. In June 1920, the Listowel (Co. Kerry) Constabu-lary were addressed by Colonel Smyth, Divisional Police Com-missioner for Munster, who in the course of his speech made some unusual recommendations.

According to a written account made subsequently by one of the policemen present, they were told that if a police barracks was burned the occupants of the nearest most convenient house

139

were to be evicted and the premises commandeered. Suspicious looking people were to be shot on sight and no policeman, they were assured, would get into trouble for making mistakes. Hunger strikers would be allowed to die and some of them, it was hinted, had already been dealt with 'in a manner their friends will never hear about'. 'Sinn Fein had had all the sport up to the present, but they were going to have the sport now.' When Smyth had finished, a policeman got up whom the men had chosen as a spokesman. 'By your accent', he said, 'I take it you are an Englishman and in your ignorance you forget you are addressing Irishmen.' The officer removed his cap, belt and sword and gave them to Smyth, saying, 'These too are English. Take them as a present from me. You are a murderer.' When Smyth ordered the man to be arrested, the other police present refused to cooperate. Similar suggestions were made at other police barracks in the South, which increased the resentment already growing amongst police to the methods employed by the Government.

As resignations from the police increased and barracks were destroyed, Collins could feel satisfied with the success of his plan. Without their 'eyes', the British were finding it impossible to govern.

Reinforcements had to be found to fill the vacant places in the R.I.C.

Chapter Twenty-Four

Early in 1920 advertisements began to appear in the British papers inviting applications for places in the Royal Irish Constabulary. The pay was to be £3.10.0 a week, all found, and previous police experience was unnecessary.

That winter Britain was experiencing the ghastly aftermath of the 1914–18 War. The streets of the cities were filled with jobless ex-soldiers who had returned from the war to find that the sacrifices they had made became irrelevant when it came to the question of steady employment. It is not difficult to imagine that in the circumstances there was an eager rush to secure jobs in the reorganized Irish Police Force. The quota was soon filled.

The first of the new police arrived in Ireland on March 25, 1920. At short notice it had not been possible to provide complete uniforms. The majority of the new recruits wore dark green constabulary caps, tunics of similar colour and khaki service trousers. A name was quickly found for them by the local population. They were called after a well-known Hunt in Limerick. The 'Black and Tans' were in business.

Three months later, another hastily recruited group joined them. These were the Auxiliaries who arrived at the end of July. The 'Auxies' were all ex-officers of the 1914–18 War and were paid £7 a week. What seems extraordinary today is the British Government's failure to comprehend at the outset what was to prove the main weakness in both organizations. Neither the 'Tans' nor the Auxiliaries were subject to military discipline.

Though the police in Ireland had always been armed, the command structure of the Force had never been designed to deal with a war situation. It was not unpredictable then that it would prove wholly inadequate when confronted with the rapidly disintegrating administration of Ireland in the summer of 1920. Quite apart from the difficulty of restraining the new 'Police', it became clear soon afterwards that the policy of the Government was to deal with terror by 'terror'. At the height of their activity the 'Black and Tans' and Auxiliaries were denounced by every Liberal paper in Britain. *The Times*, the *Manchester Guardian*, the *Daily News* and several periodicals gave detailed accounts of the 'terror campaign' authorized by the British Government from 1920 to 1921.

General Sir Hubert Gough, Commander of the Fifth Army in France, was to write, 'Law and order in Ireland have given place to a bloody and brutal anarchy, in which the armed agents of the Crown violate every law in aimless and vindictive and insolent savagery. England has departed further from her own standards and further from the standards even of any nation in the world, not excepting the Turk and Zulu, than has ever been known in history before.'

General Tom Barry has recalled what the 'Tans' were like in Cork: 'They had a special technique. Fast lorries of them would come roaring into a village, the occupants would jump out, firing shots and ordering all the inhabitants out of doors. No exceptions were allowed. Men and women, old and young, the sick and decrepit were lined up against the walls with their hands up, questioned and searched. No raid was ever carried out by them without their beating up with the butt ends of their revolvers, at least half-a-dozen people.'

The 'Auxies' were a particularly fearful looking group. Each one carried a rifle, a revolver strapped to each leg and two bombs hung from their Sam Browne belts. Within a few weeks of their coming to Ireland, the 'Auxies' began their 'scorched earth' policy. On September 20, a detachment of Auxiliaries descended on Balbriggan in Co. Meath, about fifteen miles from Dublin, and burnt the town. Seven houses were destroyed and two men bayoneted to death in the street. This was in revenge for the shooting of a Constable the day before.

On September 21, the Black and Tans burnt Tuam and Carrick-on-Shannon, two large prosperous towns in the West of Ireland. County Clare seems to have been specially singled out three days later. Ennistymon, Lahinch, Milltown Malbay were looted and houses set on fire. On September 27, Trim in Co. Meath and Mallow in Co. Cork were burned. In Mallow, £50,000 worth of damage was caused.

By far the worst burning was in Cork City. Here Tans and

Auxiliaries seem to have gone berserk. They set fire to the centre of the city, as well as important sites across the river such as the City Hall. Between two and three million pounds' worth of damage was done. Next day, the troops responsible wore burnt corks in their bonnets as a token of their 'achievement'.

Indiscriminate killing of men and women throughout the country continued on a large scale. In the beginning of November, Canon Griffin of Galway was taken out by Crown Forces and murdered. His body was later found in a bog-hole. On December 15, Canon Magner of Dunmanway, Co. Cork, was talking to a man at the corner of a street outside his Church. The Canon was not popular with the authorities as he had refused to ring his Church bells on Armistice Day, November 11. A lorry load of Auxiliaries drove up to the Canon and the man he was talking to. One of them got out and shot the man. When the Canon protested, he was shot and killed as well.

The Tans and Auxiliaries made a special target of local creameries, which showed a shrewd insight into village economy. Every village had its creamery built by the Co-operative Movement. This had been started by Sir Horace Plunkett and built up largely through the efforts of A. E. (George Russell), the poet. The aim of the Co-operative Movement was to break the grip the local merchants had on the small farmer; it would provide direct access to the markets for the farmer. The success of the Irish Co-operative Movement incited interest throughout the world and among its supporters was Henry Wallace, later Vice-President of the United States.

A. E. wrote about the attempt to destroy the organization he and Plunkett had created. 'Creameries and Mills have been burned to the ground, their machinery wrecked, agricultural stores have also been burned, property looted, boys have been killed, wounded people threatened or otherwise ill-treated. Why have these economic organizations been specially attacked? Because they have hundreds of members and if barracks have been burnt or priests have been killed or wounded in the lamentable strife now being waged in Ireland, and if the armed forces of the Crown cannot capture those guilty of the offence, the policy of reprisals condoned by the spokesmen of the Government has led to the wrecking of any enterprise in the neighbourhood, the destruction of which would inflict widespread injury and hurt the interests of the greatest number of people. I say this is being done without regard to the innocence or guilt of the persons whose property has been attacked.'

Chapter Twenty-Five

In June 1919, de Valera set out from Liverpool for the United States, smuggled on board ship. His purpose in going was to secure recognition for the Irish Republic, and to float an American loan. He arrived after eight days' voyage on the S.S. *Lappland*. His first impression of New York as he sailed into the harbour was a city of 'straw hats and sunshine'. He had left New York as a small boy of three to go back to Ireland with his mother. De Valera was still legally a United States citizen, but he told a reporter after he landed: 'When I became a soldier of the Republic I became a citizen of the Republic.'

He opened his campaign in the Waldorf Astoria on June 23 with a statement to the press. 'From today I am in America as the official head of the Republic, established by the will of the Irish people in accordance with the principles of self-determination.'

He embarked later on a colossal tour of the United States, which only a person of his physical energy and excellent health could have withstood. He addressed the Massachusetts State Legislature and was given a Civic Reception in Boston. He was made a freeman of Chicago and unveiled a statue of Robert Emmet in San Francisco. In Los Angeles twenty-five thousand people came to hear him in the Ball Park. In eight cities he had an official reception from the Governor, and in thirty-two cities he was received by the Mayor. At Cleveland, Ohio, he was greeted by hundreds of automobiles flying the tricolour and the American flag, while overhead an escort of aeroplanes flew. He received a twenty-one gun salute on entering the city. He also spoke to a joint session of the Virginia State Legislature.

While he didn't succeed in his attempt to obtain official recognition of the Irish Republic, de Valera did make Americans conscious of the Irish cause and the struggle that was going on at home. His dignified figure and calm speech were very different from the tearaway tactics associated with the Irish in the United

States. Perhaps his American origins had given him a flair for public relations. Certainly he knew how to put his image over.

De Valera's visit was to an extent marred by dissension between him and Clann na Gael, the Irish-American organization committed to the establishment of an Irish Republic and which was run by John Devoy, the Fenian. De Valera also differed with the Friends of Irish Freedom, which was led by the powerful Judge Coholan. De Valera's temperament clashed with the temperament of these Irish-Americans, and he had a number of confrontations with them which almost split the Irish-American movement. But these controversies were offset to a large extent by the extraordinary impact he made on the public throughout America. Even then it was apparent that he generated an aura of the same kind that people were later to associate with De Gaulle and Winston Churchill. Millions of people who had never met him revered him. Before he had left Ireland, his name had begun to symbolize in the minds of Europeans the message of the Irish struggle.

Now he had succeeded in capturing America in the same way. No wonder at times it had seemed to him as he went on those interminable whistle-stop tours that his exhausted larynx could never force out another word; yet when the train stopped he was always audible as he faced the crowds, dignified, pleading, captivating, with a foreign quality to heighten his Irish charm.

When de Valera returned to Ireland in January 1921 he left behind him an awareness of the Irish position that was to be of vital importance when it came to the final settlement with the British. As well, with the help of James O'Mara, a Limerick businessman whom he had brought with him to help to organize the loan, he had succeeded in raising over a million pounds for the Irish Republic.

Meanwhile, the Dail continued its policy of setting up an alternative Government in Ireland. Sinn Fein Arbitration and Land Courts were set up in May 1920. They operated in ten counties and within a year had settled four hundred cases. At the same time under Austin Stack, Minister for Justice, Republican courts with civil and criminal jurisdiction were set up. The rules of court were drawn up by young barristers from the Law

Library in Dublin's Four Courts under a leading King's Counsel, James Creed Meredith.

The Sinn Fein Supreme Court had three members who could sit as high court judges as well. Beneath this category were District and Parish Courts. The mass of the people long deprived of tribunals with which they could identify, flocked to the Sinn Fein Courts. Within a short while after they were established in June 1920, these courts operated in twenty-seven counties. The Court decrees were enforced by Republican police, who behaved with decorum and restraint, despite the absence of formal training.

Lord Monteagle, an Irish landlord, wrote to the *Irish Times* in July, 1920:

> The Sinn Fein Courts are steadily extending their jurisdiction and dispensing justice even-handed between man and man, Catholic and Protestant, farmer and shopkeeper, grazier and cattle driver, landlord and tenant. The Sinn Fein police are arresting burglars, punishing cattle drivers, patrolling the streets, controlling drink traffic, apparently in some places with the acquiescence of the local military authorities, who thus show themselves wiser than either the Castle officials or the British Government. And mark the double significance of this fact. It shows the powerlessness, in Sir Horace Plunkett's phrase, of the 'government with the dissent of the governed'. It also shows the growing and remarkable capacity of the Irish people for self-government.

The British Cabinet were well aware of the authority of these illegal courts. A friend of Walter Long, Chairman of the Irish Committee of the Cabinet, wrote to him in July, giving him a detailed account:

> I have just returned from a visit to my home in County Limerick. I found everything quite quiet. Sinn Fein rules the County – and rules it admirably. At our local races the Sinn Fein police controlled the traffic, the crowds, etc., 'parked' the motor-cars, and, in fact, did all the work which has usually been done by the police, and did it excellently. Petty thefts, or indeed crimes of any kind, are dealt with by the Sinn Fein courts, who try

the accused with perfect fairness, and administer justice in the most thorough fashion.

Here is a case for which I can vouch. A friend of mine, a lady living close by, has a very good motor-car. Three Sinn Feiners arrived, found that she was absent, told the chauffeur that they had come to take the car, that it was no good for him to offer opposition, as they were three to one and must carry out their orders; they would return it, they said, in a couple of days. They took the car – and in two days brought it back; but it was very much damaged, and they told the chauffeur that they regretted that they had an accident and had injured the car. They wrote to the owner an extremely civil letter, in which they stated that they regretted greatly having injured the car and that it had been so badly injured; but if she would send it to any garage that she chose to select in the town of Tralee, it would be thoroughly restored, put in perfect order, sent back to her, and they would, of course, pay the bill.

The fact is that everybody is going over to Sinn Fein, not because they believe in it, but because it is the only authority in the County; and they realize that if their lives and property are to be secured, they must act with Sinn Fein. Their general statement is: 'How can we avoid joining Sinn Fein when every-thing is so extremely well done?'

My friend challenged them on the murders of soldiers and police; their answer, given quietly, civilly, and deliberately, is as follows: 'These are not murders, and cannot be so described. We have declared a republic; it is true that the British Govern-ment refuses to recognize us, but that is not our affair. We have declared war against the British Government; the British Government decline for some reason of their own to recognize our act and declare war against us – but this is no affair of ours. Having declared war, we are entitled to shoot or take prisoner any soldier, policeman, or civilian, whom we believe to be actively engaged against us.'

Side by side with the operation of the Sinn Fein Courts, the Dail loan was being floated by Michael Collins. Many people had refused to pay income tax or rates, and instead sent the sums involved to Sinn Fein. Slowly the fabric of the British administration was breaking up.

Arthur Griffith's formula had been designed to break the British connection. But the principles it established would be used in different parts of the world in the future, only it would be employed under a different name, that of 'Civil Disobedience'.

Chapter Twenty-Six

Dublin by the autumn of 1920 had become an armed citadel. Curfew had been introduced. Civilians were not permitted on the streets between 8 p.m. and 5 a.m. As soon as people had retired to their houses, the military sprang to life. Lorries, tanks, armoured cars, careered through the streets. Heavy tanks lumbered up to private houses. Citizens were pulled out of bed, searched and frequently taken away to the nearest barracks.

Daily ambushes took place in the city. The area between Camden Street and George's Street became known as 'The Dardanelles', so many attacks took place there. Army lorries going down Camden Street usually had wire netting over them to deflect the grenades which might be thrown at them from the sidewalks. 'The Boers put you in lorries; the Germans put you in khaki and it took the Irish to put you in cages' one old appledealer roared at the 'Auxies' as they stopped to buy at her stall in Camden Street.[1]

Grafton Street, Dublin's fashionable thoroughfare, was in these months more like what Al Capone's Chicago was later to become. On each side of the street, tough-looking men in civilian attire walked up and down. These were the 'Igoe Gang' from Dublin Castle. This was a group of policemen who had been drafted in from the country to identify wanted men who might be visiting the city to contact I.R.A. General Headquarters.

Sometimes there would be a rush from the street as the I.R.A. Active Service moved in, summoned from their premises nearby to shoot up notorious Castle agents who had appeared. A flurry of shots, a scamper down a side alley and all that was left in the street would be a smoking body.

In the Grafton Street cafés, Auxiliary Officers used to sit drinking coffee with their revolvers on the table beside them.

[1] One of the most active in Camden Street in 1920 was the sixteen-year-old Sean McBride who would later win the Nobel Prize for Peace and the Lenin Peace Prize.

After two of them had been shot outside one café, they kept their revolvers in their right hands while they took their 'elevenses'. Why go out at all, one might ask? The Auxiliaries had a certain daring and panache. They liked social life. If they had been in Bournemouth or Brighton or Southampton, they would have gone to take coffee in the morning and they saw no reason why they shouldn't just because they happened to be in another part of what they regarded as the United Kingdom. They seemed to have a passion for photographing one another. Outside the Kodak shop in Grafton Street each day, there was sure to be a couple of lorry-loads of Auxiliaries waiting to collect their shapshots.

Many of them must have recognized by the end of 1920 that the game was up. Terror had been tried and failed. The British Press were turning against the Government. 'The Government still clings to the belief', *The Nation and Athenaeum* wrote, 'that they can crush the Irish spirit, destroy some of the bravest and most promising of Ireland's young men and win by these an outward victory. Men of noble spirit and unfaltering courage are dying but their race does not perish. We can spread ruin: that's what we are doing. We can do to Ireland just as much as Austria did to us or Germany to Belgium. The end is as certain in this case as in those, for the Irish people, supported as they are by their own spiritual vitality and the sympathy of the world, can keep this struggle alive 'till it ceases to be merely a struggle between Government and the Nation. The Government which refuses to give peace to Ireland may find sooner or later that it has broken the peace of the world.'

By this time Collins had got the upper hand in Dublin. The British knew he was winning. There was a price of £10,000 on his head. Miraculously he rode openly about the city on a bicycle on daily visits to his four offices. He had four posts – Director of Organization, Adjutant-General of the I.R.A., Director of Intelligence, and Minister of Finance in the Dail. In this latter capacity he had raised half a million pounds in Ireland in the Sinn Fein Loan. Every penny was meticulously accounted for. He had been employed as a young man in London by the Guarantee Transport Corporation of New York. The knowledge of accounting methods he acquired, he put to good use as Minister for Finance.

Collins' flair for organization enabled him to control a highly effective force of selected lieutenants. Besides conducting operations in Dublin, he kept in daily touch with I.R.A. brigades throughout the country. Hundreds of directives were issued every day. These are preserved in microfilm in the National Library of Ireland. They reflect the extraordinary gifts of a man who, sought night and day by police and military, nevertheless managed to attend to the most meticulous details of organization.

Though he had a passion for minutiae, he had none of the pettiness of the bureaucrat. He was always aware of the reality of the situation. The smallest detail was interesting to him only if it helped him to make a decision related to the overall problem at hand. To the Mid-Limerick Brigade, Collins wrote once: 'There are one hundred copies of the September number of *An tOglach* allotted to your Brigade, so that the amount due is 16/8d, please forward this sum without delay. By attending to this at once you will greatly facilitate matters.'

When he didn't get a reply, Collins wrote: '16/8d not to hand, after numerous requests. A small sum of money – agreed. Yet multiply this apparently trivial amount by, say, one hundred – what have you? A largish sum. I do not request, I insist.' On another occasion, he wrote to the same person on what seemed an unimportant detail: 'Thanks for money. Two receipts for £8 enclosed. One amount of £8 came in with a note saying it was part of First Battalion levy. Writing was not yours, but I suppose you know of it.' To a Brigade Commander, he wrote warning him to be careful of the Brigade's arms stocks: 'Flowers are important but so are guns. Without the latter, you may as well be dead. Guard what you have and guard it well.'

Though he exulted in the victories of the Flying Columns against Crown Forces, he had little time for incompetence. When Tom Barry, for instance, described the I.R.A. victory at Crossbarry to him, Collins' eyes had lit up. He was always delighted to hear of the feats of men from his native county.

On the other hand, he sent this reply to a request for rifles from County Clare: 'When you asked me for ammunition for guns which had never fired a shot in this fight, my answer is a simple one: Fire shots at some useful target or get to hell out of it.' He issued strict orders for the safety of Volunteers. 'My orders do not permit an intelligence officer to go out on night raiding parties.'

To this day there is no satisfactory explanation as to how Collins managed to avoid arrest. He walked and cycled openly about the city. At that time the geographic area of Dublin was small. Collins never moved far from the centre of it. Yet he was never recognized.

Part of his immunity to arrest seemed to stem from his audacity. Tom Barry remembers driving home to Rathgar in Dublin with Collins and some others in 1921. (Barry had come up to report to G.H.Q. about his Operations in Cork.) On the Rathgar Road, their cab was stopped by troops. To Barry's horror, Collins started to abuse them. Barry thought they were for it and prepared to make a stand. The search party seemed satisfied, however, and Collins and his party were let through. Barry, understandably shaken, criticized Collins for what he thought seemed unnecessary bravado. Collins explained to him patiently that it was by not accepting the fact that he was a wanted man that he could survive at all in Dublin.

On another occasion, Collins and Detective Eamonn Broy, his 'Castle spy', were stopped by the military at Baggot Street Bridge. 'I was terrified', Broy recalled to the author. 'Collins had his socks full of papers, with names on them and military codes. If he was caught, I was caught with them too. "O.K. Ned", he said, squeezing my leg as he got out of the car. Believe it or not if the impudent fellow didn't go straight up to the officer in charge of the search party and start to chat to him. The officer fell a victim to Mick's charm, who soon had him roaring laughing. The other soldiers, seeing Mick chatting to their commanding officer, assumed he was a friend and we were let through without examination. I was sweating but it didn't seem to take a feather out of Mick. He was chuckling all the way to Mespil Road where he was going to his office.'

One day, Collins was passing Dublin Castle to another of his offices in Crow Street, which was only a few hundred yards away. Auxiliaries jumped down off the lorries and a raid was in progress. Collins saw MacNamara, one of the detectives working for him, standing in a door just beside the Castle. MacNamara

153

nodded towards a coal lorry. Collins, taking the tip, swung a sack of coal on his shoulder and marched *into the Castle*.

The man of action had a contemplative bent. As a young man in London and later on in prison, he had read everything he could get his hands on. In an anguished moment after the Treaty in 1922, he could write to Harry Boland, his best friend who had taken sides against him, and paraphrase a passage from *Hamlet* in his letter.

Collins' incisive mind attracted Lord Birkenhead during the Anglo-Irish Treaty negotiations in 1921. Birkenhead, the Lord Chancellor, was one of the great jurists in history. He had a high regard for Collins and, writing to Churchill, he professed himself amazed at the astonishing insight of 'this former gunman' into world politics. Collins and Birkenhead became firm friends. Both were men of action with ranging minds.

Collins' statesmanlike qualities were later to be shown by his shrewd analysis of the Treaty and his assessment of what could be gained under it. History has proved Collins correct and his detractors wrong. His mind was a strange mixture of the poetic and the practical. Though he wanted the new Ireland to be self-sufficient, he is curiously modern in his determination to see that the quality of life should not perish.

He wrote in 1922, 'In the island of Achill, impoverished as the people are, hard as their lives are, difficult as the struggle for existence is, the outward aspect is a pageant. One may see processions of young women riding down on the island ponies to collect sand from the seashore, or gathering in the turf, dressed in their shawls and in their brilliantly-coloured skirts made of material spun, woven, and dyed, by themselves, as it has been spun, woven, and dyed, for over a thousand years. Their cottages also are little changed. They remain simple and picturesque. It is only in such places that one gets a glimpse of what Ireland may become again, when the beauty may be something more than a pageant, will be the outward sign of a prosperous and happy Gaelic life.'

He had an Irishman's gift for laughter and an Englishman's sense of efficiency – a formidable combination. He was a handsome Celt with well-cut features and robust physical health. Gogarty thought him 'Napoleonic, with skin like undiscoloured ivory', and gave him the key of his house to use when he was on the run.

So many gifts in one man. W. T. Cosgrave, first President of the Executive Council of the Free State and Vice-Commandant for the South Dublin Union in the 1916 Rebellion, once said to the author: 'I think Michael Collins was the greatest Irishman who ever lived, greater than Brian Boru or Parnell.'

Chapter Twenty-Seven

In the autumn of 1920, two events took place which demonstrated how completely the British administration misunderstood Ireland at this time. These events were to unleash waves of spiritual strength in the people and confirm them in their determination to resist the regime at all costs.

On October 25, Terence MacSwiney, the Lord Mayor of Cork, died on hunger strike in Brixton Prison in London. He had been without food for seventy-three days. MacSwiney had been arrested on August 17 on foot of documents found in his house, one of which was a copy of his inaugural address as Lord Mayor. Almost immediately he went on hunger strike as a protest against 'unnecessary arrests of political representatives'. Five days later he was deported to Brixton Prison near London. If the British had wanted to provide a world platform for the Lord Mayor to air his political grievances, they couldn't have done better than allow him to go on hunger strike in a British jail.

Day by day the world looked on as the Lord Mayor slowly starved to death. He was determined to resist until the Government released him unconditionally. 'It is not those who can inflict the most, but those who endure the most who will conquer', he said only a short while before he had gone to prison.

In countries other than Britain, they understood MacSwiney's action better. Throughout America, India, Russia, there was intense interest. His strike became more and more identified in the public mind with recognizable religious parallels. It was the perfect expression of the nihilist doctrine, a destruction of self that bred converts to the creed for which the sufferer had put himself on the rack. There was something about the hunger-strike of the purity of classical Russian Nihilism nourished by the Christ image and the mystical element of the religions of both peoples.

Had MacSwiney's captors taken the trouble to study his life, they could have known that he would continue to refuse food until he was released. He had written a play about a poet who had died on hunger strike rather than surrender. MacSwiney saw the National struggle in terms of a religious crusade. 'It is because', he once wrote, 'our sacrifice is akin to the sacrifice of Calvary following afar that the best and bravest of so many generations have died.'

As soon as MacSwiney became unconscious for lack of food, the waiting doctors began to feed him. But as they did, his teeth clenched to stop them even in his unaware state. Outside the prison, crowds gathered daily to pray and say the rosary. In the end, after seventy-three days without food, MacSwiney died on October 25.

As with the death of Thomas Ashe, a shudder ran through the Nation's being. The country was overwhelmed with grief. London was to see its first funeral of an Irish martyr. The Archbishop of Southwark, Dr Amigo, had given permission for his cathedral to be used for the funeral ceremony.

Irish pipers led the cortège as it passed through the streets. Mass was celebrated with the coffin of the martyred Lord Mayor on the high altar. Sir John Lavery was there to record with his brush the drama of the day. In his well-known *The Funeral of Terence MacSwiney*, the sun streams through the windows of the cathedral, lighting on the coffin, bearing witness in the centre of London to the spiritual fervour at the heart of the Irish struggle.

Down in the heart of the West country, Lady Gregory heard the news of the Lord Mayor's death from one of her county friends. 'Mrs X. called, stayed some time talking of "country newses" from the English point of view, then incidentally said, "The Lord Mayor is dead – there has been a wire." I said, "He was a brave man." She gave a superior smile. I got up and opened the window and spoke of Catherine's copybook and didn't sit down again, and she left and I looked at the hills for a while, towards the west. It is not a little thing a man to die, and he protecting his neighbour.'

One of her nephews had told Lady Gregory that it was said among the Galway county that 'Your aunt Augusta is hand and glove with the rebels.' She had been horrified at the brutalities of the troops in Galway and it was her account to Yeats of the happenings near Gort that had suggested his lines:

> Now days are dragon-ridden, the nightmare
> Rides upon sleep; a drunken soldier
> Can leave the mother murdered at her door,
> To crawl in her own blood and go scot free.

Being the woman she was, Lady Gregory didn't conceal her dislike of the Tans. Once coming out of the Abbey Theatre with some Abbey actresses, a volley rang out. Army Officers told them to put their hands up. The others fell flat on the ground but her Ladyship shouted 'Up the Rebels', in her lisping upper-class voice.

On November 1, another death took place which was to have as powerful an effect on the public mind as the death of the Lord Mayor of Cork.

On August 15, an eighteen-year-old university student named Kevin Barry had been arrested after an ambush in King Street. A soldier had been shot in the engagement and Barry was court-martialled and sentenced to death. The sentence was due to be put into effect on November 1. A powerful campaign for Barry's reprieve was launched.

While from the British point of view, Barry had been involved in killing and therefore could be hanged under the law, from an I.R.A. point of view he was a prisoner of war and should have been granted that status. Apart from this consideration nothing could be more calculated to arouse public opinion than the hanging of an eighteen-year-old student. There was also clear evidence before his execution that Barry had been tortured.

He was a particularly attractive lad, good-looking, debonair, with a gay mocking attitude towards his captors. He had been a first-class rugby player (an English game) at school and an extremely popular student in the medical school at the National University.

It is believed that Sir Henry Wilson threatened to resign as C.I.G.S. had there been a reprieve. On November 1, Kevin Barry was hanged by a British hangman in Mountjoy

Jail.[1] His name was to become the symbol throughout the world wherever young people struggle for freedom. There are few places in the English-speaking world where 'Kevin Barry' is not sung. It is, incidentally, a favourite song in the British Army and the author has heard it sung in a mess room in Gibraltar, one of the last outposts of the Empire which Barry's death was instrumental in bringing down.

> In Mountjoy Jail one Monday morning
>   High upon the gallows tree
> Kevin Barry gave his young life
>   For the cause of liberty.
>
> But a lad of eighteen summers
>   Yet there's no one can deny
> As he walked to death that morning
>   He proudly held his head on high.
>
> On that fateful Easter morning
>   In his dreary prison cell
> British soldiers tortured Barry
>   Just because he would not tell.
>
> The names of his brave companions
>   Other things they wished to know
> Turn informer or we'll hang you
>   Kevin Barry answered 'No!'

Barry's death angered many who had hoped for a settlement. Yeats was due to address the Oxford Union shortly after the execution. He spoke to a motion proposed by J. S. Collis that 'This house has no confidence in the Irish policy of the Government,'and electrified the students by leaving the platform and walking up and down among the audience waving his fists as he unleashed a tirade against the Government's misdeeds in

---

[1] A short time before the incident in Henrietta Street, Kevin Barry's mother had gone to his Battalion Commandant, Seamus Kavanagh, to ask that he be exempted from volunteer duties temporarily while he attended to his medical studies. Kavanagh had agreed and it was only on Kevin Barry's persistent pleading that he was allowed to take part in the ambush.

Ireland. The motion was passed by an overwhelming majority amid scenes of 'unexampled enthusiasm'.

A. E. had been consulted by Lord Northcliffe (the newspaper Baron and owner of *The Times*) as to what could be done to help stop the savagery. 'I was in London for a week during the years of the struggle and sought out Lord Northcliffe, who remembered that he was an Irishman. He asked me "what can I do to help?" I said he could bring American opinion to bear upon English opinion, that his vast organization would enable him to get in touch with the leaders of opinion in the United States. In less than a week he had column after column of American opinions in the papers he controlled, the voice of America's prominent statesmen, lawyers and industrialists, and it was so unanimous in favour of Irish self-government that I think it was mainly responsible for the feeling which arose in Great Britain that the Irish question was not only a domestic problem but was a world question.'

A. E.'s own writings had helped to make America aware of the Irish situation for he was well known and admired in the United States. In December 1920, A. E. contributed an essay to *Pearson's Magazine*, an American weekly, on 'The Inner and the Outer Ireland'. 'What is the root of the Irish trouble,' he wrote. 'The Irish people want to be free. Why do they desire freedom? I think it is because they feel in themselves a genius which has not yet been manifested in a civilization; as Greek, Roman and Egyptian have in the past externalized their genius in a society with culture arts and sciences peculiar to themselves.'

After describing the excesses committed by men who seemed to have been given a free hand to kill, he wrote, 'Where does the right of England to govern Ireland come from? On what is it based? Not on the will of the Irish people certainly. An ancient possession. But it is not generally conceded that a burglar who has long stolen property is the more entitled to it the longer he possesses it.'

Yeats, in a strong letter to *The Times* in December 1920, summed up the feeling which was becoming universal in Ireland, and not only in nationalist circles:

160

Dear Sir,

I read in today's *Times* that 'parties of men in four motor-lorries visited Ardrahan on Monday morning and burned dwelling-houses and other property of residents in addition to Labane parochial hall. Young men were made to run up and down the road in their night attire at the revolver point and the raids were accompanied by shooting and yelling.

Labane parochial hall was built by Mr Edward Martyn and presented to the neighbourhood for the performance of village plays. It was designed by Professor William Scott, and had a stern dignity of design. We who live in the neighbourhood had hoped that, for many years to come, it would have been the organizing centre of much popular education and much innocent pleasure. It had as much to do with politics as the extremely beautiful stained-glass presented by Mr Martyn to Labane Chapel, but perhaps I may next hear of the destruction of this glass 'accompanied by shooting and yelling'.

When the Germans were in occupation of Belgium they destroyed private houses and murdered innocent people giving the excuse that they 'had been fired on by civilians'. The English armed forces in occupation in Ireland now destroy private houses and murder innocent people in their turn giving the excuse that they have been fired on by civilians. The English Ministers who thus denounced Germany are silent.

Yours etc.,
W. B. YEATS

A vital part of the Sinn Fein programme in 1919 to 1921 was its propaganda machine. In 1919 a Government Department for Publicity had been set up. This was in the charge of Robert Brennan. Later Desmond Fitzgerald took over with Piaras Beaslai, a Dublin journalist, as a liaison with the G.H.Q. Volunteer staff. Each week the Department brought out a magazine, the *Irish Bulletin*. Over 2,000 copies went out daily to the British, Irish and foreign press, to heads of states and leading politicians in England, and to heads of Churches throughout the world. Distribution of the magazine was in itself a feat because of its illegal character. Copies had to be posted in small bundles at different letter boxes throughout the city.

The writing in the *Bulletin* was of high quality and the material chosen to attract editorial attention in the papers that it was sent to. The first Minister for Propaganda, Desmond Fitzgerald, had lived in France for some time after taking part in the 1916 Rising. He had become friendly there with Ezra Pound and Paul Eluard and was one of the founders of the Imagist Movement.

Erskine Childers, who worked for Fitzgerald and who later succeeded him as Minister for Propaganda, as the author of a best seller[1] and a former War Correspondent of *The Times*, was an admirable choice. Shortly after he had organized the Howth gun-running episode in 1914, on the outbreak of war, he had re-joined the British Army. He had had a distinguished war career winning the D.S.O. in the Royal Naval Air Service for his work in the air attack in Cuxhaven. He had become Secretary to the Irish Convention, which had been arranged by Lloyd George in 1917 to try and bring interested elements in Ireland together with a view to obtaining a form of agreement on the Home Rule Bill. Sinn Fein had boycotted this Convention and its failure had convinced Childers that the only road to freedom for Ireland was through revolution. As well as writing and editing the *Irish Bulletin*, Childers also contributed various articles to English papers, such as *The Times*, the *Manchester Guardian*, the *Daily Herald*, the *Daily Sketch*.

As someone who had been at school and university in England and had worked for most of his life there, Childers was in a position to recognize an English sense of fair play. This awareness made him particularly valuable as a propagandist. The purpose behind much of his writing was to make contact with the ordinary English man and let him know what excesses were being commit-ted in his name in Ireland by the Government.

[1] *The Riddle of the Sands*

Chapter Twenty-Eight

In the autumn of 1920, it had become clear to the General Headquarters' staff of the I.R.A. that they were confronted with a new danger.

A special intelligence unit had been organized by the British whose sole purpose was to break Collins' organization. The strategy chosen by this group was in no way complex. They intended to assassinate the political members of Sinn Fein who were moving openly in public, and who were not involved in the military struggle. Having done this, they felt that the I.R.A. would be bound to make some moves which would flush its important leaders to the surface. After September 1920, the number of raids were increased and intense searches carried out nightly in the city.

The men in charge of this organization became known as the 'Cairo Gang'. At the instigation of Sir Henry Wilson, C.I.G.S., a number of army intelligence officers had met in Cairo and planned a campaign there that would break Collins' grip on Ireland.

Henry Wilson was a man obsessed with a malign hatred for the land of his birth (he was born in Fermanagh). It was he who had been largely responsible for the introduction of the Conscription Bill in 1918. It is clear from his own diaries published after his death and from contemporary sources that he was a moving spirit behind the Curragh Mutiny in 1914, when contrary to every military convention, he had persuaded his fellow officers to refuse to accept directions from the War Office. The 'Cairo Gang' as they became known, were given carte blanche by Wilson to use any methods they might think necessary in apprehending Collins.

By October 1920, a net of intelligence agents were living in lodgings in different parts of Dublin. It is significant that, though they were regular officers, none of them belonged to any of the regiments that were stationed at that time in Dublin. These agents didn't work in the daytime; at night as soon as curfew was on, they slipped out of their lodgings in civilian clothes and accompanied raiding parties to houses in whatever area had been chosen for the night's swoop. In a surprisingly short time, they accumulated evidence which placed Collins' whole operation in great danger.

General Crozier, the Commander of the Auxiliaries, was convinced that this group were a 'Sub-rosa murder gang'. Crozier states in his autobiography that he had concluded after investigation that there was 'a police plot to do away with Sinn Fein leaders and put the blame on Sinn Fein'.

Crozier had unearthed a plot among his colleagues to murder Dr Fogarty, the Catholic Bishop of Killaloe and throw him in the Shannon at Limerick. As soon as he found out what was planned, he wrote to His Lordship who wisely went away on holiday and avoided the fate in store for him. About the same time as Crozier discovered the plot to murder the Bishop, the Lord Mayor of Limerick was murdered in his house by armed men. This group was led by a Captain Nathan, formerly of the Brigade of Guards and presumably a member of the 'Cairo Gang'. Later that night, Nathan shot and killed a former Lord Mayor of Limerick, Alderman George Clancy. (As a student, Clancy had been a close friend of James Joyce and appears in *A Portrait of the Artist as a Young Man* under the name of 'Davin'.)

On September 22, 1920, John Lynch, a Kilmallock businessman, was murdered in the Exchange Hotel, Parliament Street, Dublin. A group of men with English accents came into his room and shot him. It was established by Collins' Intelligence that one of the men responsible for Lynch's killing was a Captain Bagalley, a Court-Martial Officer who lived at 19 Eccles Street. Lynch may have been mistaken for Liam Lynch, the West Cork Brigade Leader.

In the first week in October, a plot to assassinate Arthur Griffith, then acting President of Sinn Fein, was discovered. Griffith put the facts which had been carefully sifted by Collins' Unit, to a group of pressmen in a conference held in Wynn's Hotel.

While the 'Cairo Gang' were building up their dossiers on Collins, Collins was at the same task himself in regard to them.

Liam Tobin, Tom Cullen, and Frank Thornton worked overtime sifting the information which came in. Maids employed in the boarding houses where the secret service men stayed were persuaded to save the contents of the wastepaper baskets and bring them to Collins' men. With this information before him, Collins was able to discern a coherent plan and isolate the key figures in the plot to break Sinn Fein.

One night in a raid on Vaughan's Hotel, where Collins used to meet, Liam Tobin was apprehended by a raiding party. He told such a good tale that he got away, but not before he had recognized two men whose names ran like a thread through the mass of information Collins had accumulated. These were a Lieutenant Peter Aimes, a Grenadier, who had been born in the United States, and Capt. George Bennett, formerly of the Royal Artillery.

Collins decided it was time to act. In selecting the names of the people who were to be dealt with, Headquarters' staff made every effort to see that the evidence against them was irrefutable.

General Richard Mulcahy, Chief of Staff of the I.R.A. in November 1920 is quite clear about the responsibility of those whom the I.R.A. directed their operation against on Bloody Sunday. 'They were members of a spy organization', he told the author. 'That was a murder organization. Their murderous intent was directed against the effective members of the Government as well as against the G.H.Q. and staff of the Dublin Brigade.'

On the insistence of Cathal Brugha, twenty names of men selected for assassination were turned down on grounds of insufficient evidence. A note from Collins to Dick McKee, Commandant of the Dublin Brigade, showed that the stage was set for the operation. 'Dick – have established addresses of the particular ones. Arrangements should now be made about the matter. Lieutenant G. is aware of things. He suggests the 21. Most suitable date and day I think. M.' 'Lieutenant G.' was a British Officer whom Collins had persuaded to work for the Irish cause.

On the morning of November 21, a select group of young men of the Dublin Brigade had received orders to mobilize in parts of the city. The operation they were about to undertake had been in danger of breaking down the night before.

Sean Kavanagh, Collins' Intelligence Agent for Kildare, was in Vaughan's Hotel that Saturday night when British Intelligence Officers had raided it: 'I went to the Ossory Hotel in Great Denmark Street', he told the author, 'but it was full so I went over to Vaughan's to sleep. I had no idea there was an operation on next day. Actually the whole Brigade Staff were upstairs. Then Christy Hart, the porter, went up to them in the smoke room. Christy was suspicious of a man called Edwards who was staying at the Hotel. Edwards went down to 'phone a few times. There weren't many 'phones in Dublin. Christy went in to Collins and said, "I think yez ought to be going". Mick had such trust in Christy that he just said "Let's get out of here boys". I heard Mick, Sean O'Connell and others going down the stairs. Dick McKee followed them very quickly and went out the back on his bicycle. (McKee was a tall, fine looking man, very handsome indeed, with a black moustache.) Later that night he and Peadar Clancy of the Brigade staff were discovered by the Tans and captured in a "shebeen" in the Gloucester Diamond.'

Dick McKee was the Brigade Commandant in charge of the operation and Clancy was his Vice-Commandant. After their capture they were brought to Dublin Castle and handed over to Captain King and Lieutenant Hardy, two notorious sadists, who specialized in extracting information by torture.

Collins now found himself in a terrible dilemma. If he allowed his men to go out that morning and the British had succeeded in obtaining information from McKee, the Volunteers would walk into death traps. On the other hand, if the operation did go on, and was a success, the British were even more likely to torture McKee until he told them who was responsible for the shootings. In the end, Collins decided to go on. Later, he was to maintain that he only acted 'in the nick of time', to forestall further murders.

At exactly 9.00 a.m. on Sunday morning, November 21, 1920, the firing started in different parts of the city. At 39 Upper Mount Street, an elegant Georgian boulevard with a neo-classical church at the end of it, Lieutenant Aimes and Capt. Bennett were pulled out of bed by a group of armed men and placed standing together. Both were then shot dead.

Captain Bagalley, who had been responsible for John Lynch's

death a month before, was shot by another group at 119 Lower Baggot Street. A Captain Fitzgerald met his death at 28 Earlsfort Terrace. Captain Newbury was killed at 92 Lower Baggot Street. Lieutenant Mclean, the leader of the intelligence group, was apprehended and shot at 119 Morehampton Road. Altogether fourteen spies were killed that morning. At 28 Pembroke Street, which seemed to have been a sort of Intelligence Centre, eight spies were shot. From two members of the Volunteer group, Martin Lavan (later a successful lawyer in Brighton, Michigan) and Albert Rutherford, who took part in the Pembroke Street operation, it has been possible to obtain a picture of what the killing of enemy agents on that morning involved.

After Mass, at University Church in Stephen's Green, Lavan and Rutherford gathered with twelve others outside 28 Pembroke Street. The group included George White, Charlie Dalton, Andy Cooney and a bronzed fair-haired man whom Rutherford remembered as looking like a 'Nordic hero', named Paddy Flanagan. Flanagan was a Captain in 'C' Company and, at twenty-five, was the oldest member of the group. Lavan was eighteen, Rutherford was nineteen.

They knocked on the door and a maid answered. Quietly they walked upstairs to the first landing. Here, incredibly, they waited and consulted their stop-watches. Collins had warned them not to open fire before nine o'clock. ('It's to be done exactly at nine,' he told them, 'neither before nor after. These "hoors", the British, have got to learn that Irishmen can turn up on time.')

Exactly at nine o'clock they knocked on the doors of the different people they had come to shoot. Some of the men refused to come out and were shot in bed. Others came to the door and were shot as they opened it. Two agents were shot on the landing, the stairs were running with blood. As the killings progressed, some of the younger I.R.A. men lost their nerve. Sensing this, Flanagan took four Englishmen down to the cellar and after asking their names, shot them in the side of the head. After this dreadful deed, he came upstairs and told the Volunteers to disperse without delay. The operation in Pembroke Street was complete.

Dalton took the ferry boat across the Liffey to the north side where his parents lived. Lavan and Rutherford went to play a football match at Dolphin's Barn about a mile away. They had taken the precaution the night before of having their names put in the paper as playing for a team called the 'Mickey Malones'.

Bill Stapleton and Joe Leonard of the Squad had been in charge at 92 Lower Baggot Street. 'Captain Newbury heard us coming and locked the door,' Stapleton recalled to the author. 'He was in bed with his wife. His room was on the ground floor at the left as you went in the door. It had been identified by an Intelligence Officer who was with us when we shot our way in. The unfortunate man was half way out of the window, but we fired at him as he straddled it.'

By 9.30 a.m. the killing everywhere was over. As yet the military were not aware of what had happened. At about 9.20 a.m., General Crozier was passing 22 Upper Mount Street with a group of Auxiliaries when they heard shooting. It was probably the execution of a spy named McMahon, who had been warned more than once by Collins not to come back to Ireland. Crozier jumped out and ran towards the house. Two Auxiliaries who went to the back were shot by Tom Keogh who burst out through the soldiers as they surrounded him. When he had arrived at 22 Upper Mount Street, Keogh had made a date with the servant maid who answered, before he went upstairs. When he found himself surrounded he said to a friend, 'I've got to keep that date' and proceeded to shoot his way out. After Crozier had seen what happened upstairs, he went down to the garden where he found an Auxiliary about to shoot Frank Teeling, one of Collins' men. Crozier knocked the revolver out of the Auxiliary's hand and, after having seen to it that Teeling was taken to hospital, drove down to the city centre and went into Dublin Castle. He seems to have enjoyed the chagrin of the officers when they heard what was happening outside. As a former regular army officer, Crozier felt that if a spy was shot, it was part of the game. He heard a horror-stricken officer, coming back from the telephone, say, 'About fifty officers have been shot. Collins has done in most of the Secret Service people.'

Throughout the city that morning, anxious men could be seen leaving lodgings and hurrying towards Dublin Castle with their baggage. They knew the game was up. Actually Collins' men had been out to get twenty that morning but only ten of them had been at home.

Volunteer Joe Dolan of C Company, 3rd Battalion, had gone to a house in Ranelagh to shoot a Lieutenant King. 'He wasn't there,' Dolan told the author, 'but I found his paramour. I was so angry I gave the poor girl a right scourging with the sword scabbard. Then I set the room on fire.'

Lloyd George hadn't much sympathy for the dead men. 'They got what they deserved. Beaten by counter jumpers,' he told Mr P. Moylett, an Irish businessman, a few weeks after the event.

This, however, was not how the matter was presented the following week to the British public and to the world at large. The 'murdered officers' were given a State funeral in London. The Catholic dead had been taken to Westminster Cathedral while the others were taken to Westminster Abbey for Requiem service. The procession through the streets of London was led by brass bands of the Brigade Guards and Household Cavalry. The coffins were in gun carriages and detachments of police marched on either side.

Britain was horrified. The *Evening News* wrote: 'I wonder again if one of the guilty men is among the scattering crowd, with the blood reeking on his hands and the stench of foul murder rising from his heart. I wonder if this man trembles and grows faint as he knows secretly that the furies, the dark maidens with serpents twining in their hair, and black blood dripping from their eyes, are following him and hunting him, hounding him on to an awful and bloody end.'

At O'Connell Bridge in Dublin, Sean Kavanagh stood with Tobin, Gearoid O'Sullivan and other members of the Brigade Staff as the long line of gun carriages bearing the coffins, draped in the Union Jack, passed by. Hats and caps were floating down the Liffey knocked off the heads of by-standers by policemen. Frank Hugh O'Donnell spoke out of the corner of his mouth to Kavanagh to go up to the King George V Hospital and claim Dick McKee's body. McKee and Clancy had been killed after prolonged torture on Sunday in Dublin Castle, having refused to give information about the events that had occurred that morning. Kavanagh followed out the order in company with Ben

Ryan who was later captured and hung for his part in Bloody Sunday.

A few days later Bill Stapleton of the Squad got an order to go down to the Dublin kips. This was the brothel area of Dublin, famous as the scene of the 'Circe Episode' in Joyce's *Ulysses*. He had instructions to deal with the man who had betrayed McKee and Clancy to the authorities. 'The spy turned out to be Becky Cooper's "fancy man". She was a well-known Madam. We found him in a pub, a big burly man. He blustered at first: then we took him out and shot him.'

An event which took place on the afternoon of the day of the killings seems to have made little impression in Britain. A detachment of Black and Tans went to Croke Park Sports Ground, Dublin at 3.15 p.m. where an inter-county Gaelic Football Match was in progress. Ostensibly the Tans were there to support a search for arms that was to be made among the crowd by the Army.

But that their purpose was a grimmer one was soon clear. Stationed on a railway bridge at one end of the ground, a group of Tans fired a machine gun at random into the crowd. People panicked immediately and ran onto the field. But the firing continued. Dead and wounded were lying all over the pitch. One of the players wearing his green and gold jersey had a bullet put through his forehead. In fact, the presence of the Army as opposed to the Tans probably avoided further massacres. A drunken Black and Tan had lined the teams up and was walking up and down in front of them with a revolver in his hand. An Army officer came over and whispered to one of the team. 'He means to finish you all off.' The officer then went over to the Tan and persuaded him to go away. The actual casualties that day were twelve dead and seventy wounded.

When the subject of the 'murdered officers' was raised a few days after Bloody Sunday in the House of Commons, the Croke Park shootings were not referred to at all. After Sir Hamar Greenwood, the Under Secretary of State for Ireland, had described in hushed silence, 'The cruel and savage massacre and wounding of an armed British officer', Joe Devlin, Member of Parliament for West Belfast, rose and asked if the Honourable Member had no knowledge of the appearances of Her Majesty's forces on the football field? A Major Morrison jumped on Devlin's shoulders and tried to pull him down. Other members shouted, 'Kill him, kill him.'

Parliament was in a state of shock. It found itself confronted with the effects of a new military phenomenon, to which it was impossible to apply the normal rules of war. Bloody Sunday was the day that British Rule broke in Ireland. It was the fruition of Collins' plan 'to put out the eyes of the British' by annihilating their intelligence corps. From this time forward British Government in Ireland was paralyzed.[1]

Any events which occurred after November 1920 were insignificant compared to the effect that Bloody Sunday had on those who governed Ireland. Collins knew this and later was to say he could have had a Truce with the British at Christmas 1920 (instead of July 1921) if it hadn't been for the interference of well-meaning peace-makers.

Not only was Bloody Sunday to mark the end of Britain's rule in the greater part of Ireland, it was to be the beginning of the break-up of British rule throughout the Empire.

In Kenya, in Cyprus, in Egypt, Palestine and Burma, for the next forty years, guerilla leaders were to claim Collins as their prototype and adapt the strategy he had designed for evacuating the colonial power.

Collins himself had no doubt that he had done the right thing. Later he was to write: 'My one intention was the destruction of the undesirables who had continued to make miserable the lives of ordinary, decent citizens. I have proof enough to assure myself of the atrocities which this gang of spies and informers have

[1] In April, 1921, Tom Jones, Lloyd George's private secretary, wrote to Bonar Law: 'Where was Michael Collins during the Great War? He would have been worth a dozen brass hats. Can't you get him to spend the weekend with you in France unofficially. I am sure the Prime Minister has a secret admiration for him.'

Sir William Darling, who met Collins a little later, was struck by his knowledge of military tactics and his martial spirit in expressing admiration for the courage of some of the Tans. Darling also discovered Collins' literary leanings, noting that he could recite Whitman at will and his fascination for G. K. Chesterton's 'Napoleon of Notting Hill', which it seems, made a deep impression on him.

committed. Perjury and torture are words too easily known to them.

'If I had a second motive, it was no more than a feeling such as I would have for a dangerous reptile.

'By their destruction the very air is made sweeter. That should be the future's judgment on this particular event. For myself, my conscience is clear. There is no crime in detecting and destroying in war-time the spy and the informer. I have destroyed without trial. I have paid them back in their own coin.'

Collins' best friend had been killed on Bloody Sunday. He had proceeded with the operation knowing that Dick McKee would never betray the Volunteers under torture.

Now when McKee's body was laid out in Dublin's Pro-Cathedral, Collins was one of those who helped to arrange the body. He brought along his own Volunteer uniform and put it on the body of his dead friend. It was a soldier's tribute. No power on earth could have prevented Collins attending, though he must have taken an appalling risk walking about openly in the centre of the city at a ceremony where G men and Military would have been on the look-out for wanted men.[1]

Meanwhile, the British authorities in a frenzy raged through Dublin, looking for 'the murderer', Michael Collins.

It was the fury of the impotent.

[1] On Bloody Sunday night Collins had gone as usual for dinner to the O'Donovans' house at 5 Airfield Road, Rathgar. Next day he attended a wedding and had his photograph taken with the wedding group. (Related to the author by members of the O'Donovan family.)

Epilogue

In January 1922, a year and two months after Bloody Sunday, the British Army marched down the Quays of Dublin and left the country. The Union Jack was hauled down from Dublin Castle and replaced by the Tricolour of the new Irish State.

Michael Collins arrived in a taxi to take over on behalf of the provisional government from the last Viceroy, Lord Fitzalan. 'I am glad to see you, Mr Collins', the Viceroy said, holding out his hand. 'Like hell you are', said Collins with a grin.

The previous summer, the British, out-manoeuvred by Collins' tactics, had agreed to a truce. Sinn Fein was given belligerent status, de Valera began negotiations with Lloyd George and between September and December of 1921 plenipotentiaries from the Dail were dispatched to London to negotiate terms.

A Treaty was accepted by the Dail in January and immediately the British administration began to move out. The six North Eastern counties, however, were to remain within the United Kingdom; but a clause had been inserted in the Treaty which seemed to ensure that two of these counties would join the new State in a year or two and it was assumed the other four would merge before long.

Sinn Fein had divided on the terms of the Treaty. A majority led by Michael Collins and Arthur Griffith had voted to work it. A short bitter conflict between the two parties ended after nine months in May 1922 when the newly elected Government proceeded to set up institutions of state. By this time Collins and Griffith were dead, Collins killed in the civil conflict, Griffith dead from a stroke.

A mild looking little man with blue eyes and golden hair, W. T. Cosgrave, became President after Griffith's death. He had been sentenced to death in 1916 as Vice-Commandant of the South Dublin Union but his sentence was later commuted to life imprisonment. Cosgrave turned out to have a steel-like quality and his courage and resolution were largely responsible for holding the young State together during its early years.

A Senate was formed which included a number of representatives from the landed gentry. Griffith's policy had been to utilize all sections of the community in the running of the country and his offer to 'come and get the country under way' was well received by Protestant Unionists.

The Earl of Granard, Sir Hutchinson Poe, Sir Thomas Esmonde and Lord Dunraven, were among those who became Free State Senators. The first Chairman of the Senate was Lord Glenavy who as Sir James Campbell had been Carson's ally in 1912. Andrew Jameson, the leader of the Irish Unionists, was another who accepted the invitation to become a Senator. W. B. Yeats and Oliver St John Gogarty were among those nominated for literary achievement. Yeats was made Chairman of a committee set up to produce a new Irish coinage, and a very handsome job he made of it, selecting Charles Ricketts, the English painter, to do the designs.

In 1927, de Valera, who at first refused to recognize the new Parliament, was now persuaded to accept its authority. He and his followers entered the Dail on May 20 of that year.

Five years later in the General Election of 1932, his party (known as Fianna Fail) was returned to power. As soon as he was in Government, de Valera set about dismantling the remnants of the Imperial connection. Ironically, he was enabled to do this by the provisions of the Statute of Westminster whose enactment had been secured largely by the efforts of two of his opponents, Kevin O'Higgins and Patrick McGilligan at the Imperial Conference in 1926. This provided that a Dominion could legislate independently of Westminster and was to prove a virtual charter to republicanism.

De Valera removed the oath of allegiance to the King, dissolved the post of Governor General, and in 1937, took advantage of the Abdication crisis to pass the new constitution. In 1938, he had a major political triumph when he persuaded the British Government to evacuate the three Ports which they still held under the terms of the Treaty on Irish territory. With Britain finally out, it was not difficult to maintain a neutral stance during the Second World War. De Valera's attitude, and it was one shared by a majority of Irishmen, was that so many had died helping Britain in the first war in expectation of a Home Rule Bill which was never passed, that in the second one the Irish were entitled to abstain and concentrate on the building up of the young State.

In 1948, de Valera's Government was defeated and a Coalition came to power. One of the first things the new Government did was to pass the Republic of Ireland Act which finally removed Ireland from the Commonwealth.

Those who supported the stand of the first Free State Government in accepting the Treaty with Britain after the Anglo-Irish war, felt with the passing of the Republic of Ireland Act that the settlement had been justified. It had given 'freedom to achieve freedom'.

Presently the Republic of Ireland is a member of the United Nations Assembly and one of the nine European countries in the EEC. Its economy is a mixed one, based on agriculture, tourism and foreign investment. Parliamentary democracy has survived, despite threats from the right and left, and there is stable government. The legal system is based on the English one that it replaced and functions very much on the same lines, except that judicial decisions are subject to the articles of a written Constitution. Self-Government has left citizens of a twenty-six county republic free to develop their identity so that they can look on the sister island with a clearer eye. This congenial result has assisted those who argue that colonial government of Ireland inhibited proper development of the country's resources.

It has been otherwise in the north-east corner of the country. The hopes of those who signed the Treaty – that it would lead to an all-Ireland Parliament and the removal of the British presence from the island – have not been fulfilled, and the six counties of contention have remained part of the United Kingdom. A local parliament, Stormont, established in Belfast, instituted a system of rigid privilege with the intention of keeping the Nationalist minority in an inferior position. One result of this is that in the first fifty years of government, there was not one Catholic in the Northern Ireland Cabinet.

The *Sunday Times* Insight Team in 1971 assessed the main weakness of partition. 'The border was itself the first and biggest gerrymander. Those counties it enclosed in the new province of Ulster had no point or meaning, except as the largest area which the Protestant tribe could hold against the Catholics. Protestant supremacy was the only reason why the State existed. As such the State itself was an immoral concept.'

It had its genesis in an illegal act by a governing class who had refused to accept the Rule of Law in 1914, climaxing in the mutiny of the Army officers of the Curragh when ordered by the Cabinet to confront the unlawful activities of the Unionists in Northern Ireland. Established on such foundations, it is not surprising that the process appears to be a continuing one. In 1974 the Northern Ireland Assembly which was made up of a coalition of Unionists and Nationalist politicians was brought down by the failure of the Government to deal with illegal actions by the Ulster Workers' Council and collusion between the security forces and Loyalist paramilitaries. As Robert Fisk wrote in his masterful *The Point of No Return*, viewed from Dublin this breach of the Rule of Law 'smacked of that old spectral insurrection of the Curragh and the outrage which this engendered even among moderate nationalist opinion was demonstrated in the *Irish Times* leader the following day.' The leader Fisk quotes from ends with: 'In all the shame Britain has suffered at the hands of her departing colonialists this lying down to the bigots of Belfast ranks high in infamy.' (*Irish Times*, 25 May 1974.)

Again in 1987 the Government appeared to fail to operate the Rule of Law when they refused to accept the report of Assistant Chief Constable Stalker on the alleged shoot to kill policy of the security forces in Northern Ireland. Perhaps the most powerful indication that matters had not changed at the root of power was the release of Private Ian Thain in February 1988 after serving only three and a half years of a life sentence for the murder of a Northern Ireland civilian. After his return to his unit, it was revealed that despite his conviction, Private Thain had never ceased to be a serving member of the army.

Fisk's book underlines the subtle collusion between Army, landed gentry, sympathetic members of the government and a commercial elite which will ensure that working-class Loyalists can confront with impunity the Rule of Law. It is the classic colonial position. Had this powerful combination or establishment relaxed its position at an earlier stage and assisted the course of progress, the relations between the two islands today could have been different.

One occasion in particular stands out when there was a chance of real progress if a generous gesture was made, namely when Major Willie Redmond, M.C. (a brother of John Redmond, the Irish leader) spoke to the House of Commons in March 1917. He had come back from the front line of France to second a motion for immediate Home Rule and was still dressed in his trench-stained uniform as he addressed the House:

> I want to speak to those Irish soldiers I have left in France, and if they could all speak with one voice and with one accord they would say to this House, to men in every part of it, to Conservatives, Liberals and Labour men, to their Nationalist countrymen and to their countrymen from the North of Ireland, in the name of God we here who are about to die, perhaps, ask you to do that which largely induced us to leave our homes; to do that which our fathers and mothers taught us to long for; to do that which is all we desire, make our country happy and contented, and enable us when we meet the Canadians and the Australians and the New Zealanders, side by side in the common cause and the common field to say to them, 'Our country, just as yours, has self-government.'

Willie Redmond (aged 54) was killed three months later in the Great Push. My uncle (aged 19), a Lieutenant in the Royal Munster Fusiliers, was killed in the same battle. He, no doubt, would have supported Willie Redmond's appeal, as would the 49,000 other Nationalist Irishmen who died in the Great War, fighting for Britain. How much bloodshed could have been saved if those words had been listened to and Home Rule granted before it was too late and Irishmen in their own country were driven to violence to redeem the broken pledge.

Select Bibliography

A. E. (George Russell). *The Inner and Outer Ireland*. Published in *Pearson's Magazine*. U.S.A.

Abels, Jules. *The Parnell Tragedy*. London 1966

Anderson, R. A. *With Horace Plunkett in Ireland*. London

Barry, Tom. *Guerilla Days in Ireland*. Dublin 1949

Bax, Arnold. *Farewell My Youth*. London 1943

Beaslai, Piaras. *Michael Collins and the Making of a New Ireland*. 2 vols. London 1926

Beckett, J. C. *A Short History of Ireland*. London 1952

Bennett, Richard. *The Black and Tans*. Great Britain 1959

Blunt, Wilfred. *My Diaries*. Foreword by Lady Gregory. 2 vols. London 1919–20

Bourke, Marcus. *John O'Leary*. Dublin 1968

Boyce, D. G. *Englishmen and Irish Troubles*. London 1972

Boyce, D. G. *Nationalism in Ireland*. Dublin 1982

Bowyer, Bell, J. *The Secret Army: The IRA 1916–79*. Dublin 1979

Breen, Dan. *My Fight for Irish Freedom*. Dublin 1950

Brennan, John. *The Years Flew By*. Recollections of Sydney Gifford Czira. Dublin 1974

Brennan, M. *The War in Clare 1911–21*. Dublin 1980

Brennan, Robert. *Allegiance*. Dublin 1950

Briolly, Sylvain. *Ireland in Rebellion*. Dublin 1922

Bromage, Mary C. *De Valera and the March of a Nation*. London 1956

Butler, Ewan. *Barry's Flying Column*. Great Britain 1971

Callwell, Major-General Sir C. E. *Field Marshall Sir Henry Wilson, His Life and Diaries*. 2 vols. London 1927; *The Capuchin Annual*. London 1967; *The Capuchin Annual*. London 1969

Cardozo, Nancy. *Maud Gonne*. London 1978

Cashman, D. B. *The Life of Michael Davitt*. London

Caulfield, Max. *The Easter Rebellion*. London 1964

Chadwick, Nora. *The Celts*. London 1970

Churchill, Winston S. *The Aftermath* (Vol. V of *The World Crisis*). London 1929; *Thoughts and Adventures*. London 1932; *Step by Step 1936–39*. London 1939

Clarke, Austin. *A Penny in the Clouds*. London 1968

Clarke, Thomas J. *Glimpses of an Irish Felon's Prison Life*. London 1922

Coffey, Diarmid. *Douglas Hyde, President of Ireland*. Dublin 1938

Colum, Padraic. *Arthur Griffith*. Dublin 1959

Collins, Michael. *The Path to Freedom*. Cork 1968

Colvin, Ian. *The Life of Edward Carson*. Vol 2. London 1934

Connolly, James. *Labour in Ireland*. London and Dublin 1922

Coogan, Tim Pat. *Ireland Since the Rising*. London 1968; *The I.R.A.* Dublin 1988

Corfe, Tom. *The Phoenix Park Murders*. London 1968

Coughlan, Anthony. *The Way to Peace in Ireland*. Ireland

Coxhead, Elizabeth. *Daughters of Erin*. London 1965

Cronin, Sean. *The Revolutionaries*. Dublin 1971; *The McGarrity Papers*. Ireland 1972

Crozier, Brigadier F. P. *Impressions and Recollections*. London 1930; *Ireland For Ever*. London 1932

Czira, Mme Sydney. *The Years Flew By*. Dublin 1974

Dail Eireann. December 1921-January 1922

Dalton, Charles. *With the Dublin Brigade 1917–21*. London 1929

Daly, Dominic. *The Young Douglas Hyde*. Dublin 1973

Davis, Richard. *Arthur Griffith and Non-Violent Sinn Fein*. Ireland 1974

Davitt, Michael. *The Fall of Feudalism in Ireland*. London and New York 1904

Deasy, Liam. *Towards Ireland Free* (ed. John E. Chisholm). Dublin and Cork 1973

de Burca, Seamus. *The Soldiers Song*. Dublin 1957

de Vere White, Terence. *A Leaf from the Yellow Book*. London 1958; *Kevin O'Higgins*. London 1948

Devoy, John. *Recollections of an Irish Rebel*. New York 1929

Digby, Margaret. *Horace Plunkett, An Anglo-American Irishman*. Oxford 1949

Duff, Charles. *Six Days to Shake an Empire*. London 1966

Duff, Douglas. *The Rough with the Smooth*. London 1940

Edwards, R. D. and Williams, T. D. (editors). *The Great Famine*. Dublin 1956

Eglinton, John. *A Memoir of A. E.* London 1937

Ervine, St John. *Craigavon*. London 1949

Ervine, St John. *Irishmen of Today, Edward Carson*. Dublin 1915

Fanon, Frantz. *The Wretched of the Earth*. London 1967

Figgis, Darrel. *Recollections of the Irish War*. London 1927

Fingall, Elizabeth, Countess of. *Seventy years Young*. London

Fischer, Louis. *Gandhi*. New York 1954; *The Essential Gandhi* (edited by Fischer). New York 1962

Fisher, T. *The Revival of Irish Literature*. (With Sir Charles Gavan Duffy and George Sigerson). London 1894

Fisk, Robert. *The Point of No Return*. London 1975

Fitzgerald, Desmond. *Memoirs*. London 1969

Fitzgibbon, Constantine. *The Life and Times of Eamon de Valera*. Dublin 1973

Forester, Margery. *Michael Collins – The Lost Leader*. London 1971

Forster, E. M. *A Passage to India*. U.S.A. 1924; *The Hill of Devi*. New York 1953; *Maurice*. London 1971

Foster, R. F. *C. S. Parnell: The Man and his Family*. U.S.A. 1976

Friel, Brian. *Collected Plays*. London 1984

Gandhi the Man. Compiled from the perspective of Eknath Easwaran of the Blue Mountain Centre of Meditation by Jo Anne Black, Nick Harvey and Laurel Robertson. San Francisco 1973

Gallagher, Frank (pseud. David Hogan). *The Four Glorious Years*. Dublin 1953

Gaucher, Roland. *The Terrorists*. London 1968

Gaughan, J. A. *Austin Stack: Portrait of a Separatist*. Dublin 1977

Gibbon, Monk. *Inglorious Soldiers*. London 1968

Gleeson, James. *Bloody Sunday*. Great Britain 1962

Gogarty, Oliver St John. *As I was Going Down Sackville Street; It Isn't This Time of Year at All*. London 1954

Gray, Tony. *The Orange Order*. London 1972

Great Irishmen. By John E. Redmond, T. P. O'Connor, M. P. Joseph Keating, Capt. Stephen L. Gwynn and D. Polson. London 1920

Greaves, Desmond C. *The Life and Times of James Connolly*. London 1961; *Liam Mellows and the Irish Revolution*. London 1971

Gregory, Lady. *Ideals in Ireland*. London 1901

Gregory, Lady. *Seventy years: Being an Autobiography*. New York 1974

Gwynn, Denis. *Edward Martyn and the Irish Revival*. London 1930; *Life of John Redmond*. London 1932; *De Valera*. London 1933

Haverty, Ann. *Constance Markievicz, An Independent Life*. London 1988

Headlam, Maurice. *Irish Reminiscences*. London 1947

Healy, T. M. *Letters and Leaders of My Day*. 2 vols. London 1928

Holt, Edgar. *Protest in Arms*. London 1960

Hopkinson, Michael. *Green Against Green; The Irish Civil War*. Dublin 1988

Horgan, John J. *Parnell to Pearse*. Dublin 1949

Hone, J. M. *The Life of George Moore*. London 1936; *W. B. Yeats 1865–1939*. London 1962

Howarth, Herbert. *The Irish Writers 1880–1940*. London 1958

Hyde, Montgomery. *The Trial of Roger Casement*. London 1960

Hyde, Montgomery. *Carson*. London 1974

Inglis, Brian. *The Story of Ireland; Roger Casement*. London 1973

Ireland, Denis. *Patriotic Adventurer*. London 1936

Irish Times: Sein Fein Rebellion Handbook: Easter 1916

Jones, Thomas. *Whitehall Diary*. London 1971

Joyce, Stanislaus and Mason, Ellsworth (editors). *The Early Joyce – The Book reviews 1902–03*. U.S.A. 1955

Kee, Robert. *The Green Flag*. London 1972

Kettle, T. M. (editor). *Irish Orators and Oratory*. Dublin

Kettle, T. M. *A Note on Sein Fein in Ireland. North American Review vol CLXXXVII*. U.S.A. 1908

Kiberd, Declan. *Synge and the Irish Language*. London 1979

King, Clifford. *The Orange and the Green*. Great Britain 1965

Larkin, Emmet. *James Larkin*. London 1968

Lavelle, Patricia. *James O'Mara: A Staunch Sein Feiner*. Dublin 1961

Lazenby, Elizabeth. *Ireland – A Catspaw*. London 1928; *Lenin on Ireland*. Dublin 1970

Lennon, C. *Richard Stanihurst (1547–1618) and Old English Identity. Irish Historical Studies*. Vol XXI. Dublin 1978

Le Roux, L. N. *Patrick Pearse*. Dublin 1932

Levenson, S. *James Connolly, A Biography*. London 1973

Longford, the Earl of and O'Neill, T. P. *Eamon de Valera*. London 1970

Longford, Elizabeth. *A Pilgrimage of Passion*. London 1979

Linklater, Andro. *An Unhusbanded Life, Charlotte Despard, Suffragette, Socialist and Sinn Feiner*. London 1980

Lynch, D. *The I.R.B. and the 1916 Rising*. Cork 1957

Lyons, F. S. L. *John Dillon*. London 1968

Lyons, F. S. L. *Charles Stuart Parnell*. London 1977

Lyons, George. *Some Recollections of Griffith and His Times*. Dublin 1923

Macardle, Dorothy. *The Irish Republic*. Dublin 1937

MacEoin, U. (editor). *Survivors*. Dublin 1981

MacBride, Maud Gonne. *A Servant of the Queen*. Great Britain 1938

MacCarthy, J. M. (editor). *Limerick's Fighting Story*. Ireland

MacColl, Rene. *Roger Casement*. London 1956

MacDonagh, Michael. *The Irish at the Front*. London 1916

MacEntee, Sean. *Episode at Easter*. Dublin 1966

MacLysaght, Edward. *Irish Life in the Seventeenth Century*. Ireland 1950

MacManus, Francis (editor). *The Years of the Great Test 1936–39*. Cork 1967

MacManus, M. J. *Eamon de Valera*. Dublin 1944

MacPhiarais, Padraig. *O pheann an Phiarsaigh*. Dublin

Macready, The Rt Hon. Sir Nevil. *Annals of An Active Life*. Vols I & II. London.

Madden, Daniel O. *Grattan's Speeches*. Dublin 1867

Manning, Maurice. *The Blueshirts*. Dublin 1970

Mansergh, Nicholas. *The Irish Question 1840–1921*. London 1965

Marjoribanks, Edward. *The Life of Lord Carson*. Vol 1. London 1934

Marreco, A. *The Rebel Countess*. London 1967

Martin, F. X. (editor) *Leaders and Men of the Easter Rising: Dublin 1916*. London 1967; *The Scholarly Revolutionary: Eoin MacNeill 1867–1945, and the Making of Ireland*. Ireland 1973

Martin, Hugh. *Insurrection in Ireland*. London 1921

McCann, Eamonn. *War and an Irish Town*. London 1974

McDonagh, Thomas. *Literature in Ireland*. Dublin 1916

McHugh, Roger. *Dublin 1916*. London 1966

McInerney, Michael. *The Riddle of Erskine Childers*. Dublin 1971

Middleton, K. P., the Earl of. *Records and Reactions 1856–1939*. London 1939

Monteith, Capt. Robert. *Casement's Last Adventure*. Dublin 1953

Moore, George. *Hail and Farewell*. 3 vols. London 1937

Morley, Henry. (editor). *Ireland Under Elizabeth and James I*. London 1890

Morley, John. *Life of Gladstone*. London 1903

Neeson, Eoin. *The Civil War in Ireland 1922–23*. Cork 1967; *The Life and Death of Michael Collins*. Cork 1968

Neligan, David. *The Spy in the Castle*. London 1968

Nevinson, Henry, W. *Visions and Memories*. London 1944

Nicolson, Sir Harold. *King George V*. London 1944

Nowlan, K. B. (editor). *The Making of 1916*. Dublin 1969

O'Bourke, Marcus. *John O'Leary: A Study in Separation*. Dublin 1967

O'Brien, Conor Cruise. *Parnell and His Party 1880–92*. 2 vols. London 1957; (editor) *The Shaping of Modern Ireland*. London 1959

O'Brien, R. Barry. *The Life of Charles Stuart Parnell 1846–91*. 2 vols. London 1898

O'Brien, Nora Connolly. *Portrait of a Rebel Father*. London 1935

O'Brien, William. *The Parnell of Real Life*. London 1926

O'Broin, Leon. *Dublin Castle and the 1916 Rising*. London 1966; *The Prime Informer*. London 1971

O Buachalla, Seamus. *The Letters of P. H. Pearse*. London 1980

O'Callaghan, Sean. *The Easter Lily*. London 1956; *Execution*. London 1974

O'Casey, Sean. *Drums Under the Window*. London 1945; *Inishfallen Fare Thee Well*. London 1949. *Pictures in the Hallway*. London 1963

O'Connor, Batt. *With Michael Collins in the Fight for Irish Independence*. London 1929

O'Connor, Frank. *The Big Fellow*. U.S.A. 1937

O'Connor, the Rt Hon. Sir James. *History of Ireland 1798–1924*. Vol I. London 1925

O'Donnell, P. *The Gates Flew Open*. Cork 1965

O'Donoghue, Florence. *No Other Law*. Dublin 1954; *Thomas MacCurtain*. Ireland 1955

O'Faolain, Sean. *Constance Markievicz*. London 1934; *King of the Beggars*. London 1938; *De Valera*. London 1939

O'Fearail, Padraig. *The Story of Conradh na Gaeilge*. Dublin 1971

O'Hegarty, P. S. *A History of Ireland Under the Union 1809–1922*. London 1952

O'Leary, John. *Recollections of Fenians and Fenianism*. London 1896. Ireland 1968

O'Luing, Sean. *I Die in a Good Cause*. Ireland

O'Malley, Ernie. *On Another Man's Wound*. London 1936

O'Malley, Ernie. *The Singing Flame*. Ireland 1978

O'Neill, T. P. (editor). *The Anglo-Irish Treaty*.

O'Sullivan, Donal. *The Irish Free State*. London 1940

O'Sullivan, Seumas. *Essays and Recollections*. Dublin 1944

O'Tuama, Sean. *The Gaelic League Idea*. Cork 1972

Pearse, Padraic H. *Plays, Stories, Poems*. Dublin; *Political Writings and Speeches*. Dublin 1962

Plunkett, Horace. *Ireland in the New Century*. London 1905

Redmond, Major William, M. P. *Trench Pictures from France*. London 1917

Renan, E. *What is a Nation?* (From *The Poetry of the Celtic Races and Other Studies of Ernest Renan*). London 1896

Riddell, Lord. *More Pages from my Diary*. Published by *Country Life*. London 1934

Robinson, the Rt Hon. Henry. *Memories: Wise and Otherwise*. London 1923

Robinson, Lennox. *Bryan Cooper*. London 1931

Rolleston, C. H. *Portrait of an Irishman*. London 1939

Russell, Diarmuid (selected and edited by). *The Portable Irish Reader*. New York 1946

Ryan, A. P. *Mutiny at the Curragh*. London 1956

Ryan, Desmond. *The Man Called Pearse*. Dublin 1919; *James Connolly, His Life, Work and Writings*. Dublin 1924; *Remembering Sion*. London 1934; *Unique Dictator*. London 1934; *The Rising: The Complete Story of Easter Week*. 3rd edition. Dublin 1957; *Sean Treacy and the Third Tipperary Brigade*. Dublin 1962

Ryan, Mark. *Fenian Memories*. Dublin 1945

Shakespeare, Sir Geoffrey. *Let Candles Be Brought In*. London 1949

Shaw, George Bernard. *The Matter With Ireland*. London 1962

Shiubhlaigh, Maire Nic. *The Splendid Years*. Recollections as told to Edward Kenny. Dublin 1955

Spindler, Karl. *The Mystery of the Casement Ship*. Berlin 1931

Stephens, James. *The Insurrection in Dublin*. Dublin and London 1916

Steward, A. T. Q. *The Ulster Crisis*. London 1967

Stewart, A. T. Q. *Edward Carson*. Dublin 1981

Sunday Times Insight Team. *Ulster*. London 1972

Swift, Jonathan. *A Short View of the State of Ireland*. Dublin 1728

Taafe, Michael. *Those Days are Gone Away*. London 1959

Taber, Robert. *The War of the Flea*. Great Britain 1970

Taylor, Rex. *Michael Collins*. Great Britain 1970

Tery, Simone. *En Irlande*. Paris 1923

Tierney, Michael. *Eoin MacNeill: Scholar and Man of Action 1867–1945*. Oxford 1981

Van Voris, Jacqueline. *Constance de Markievicz*. New York 1972

Venturi, Franco. *Roots of Revolution*. London 1960

Woodham-Smith, Cecil. *The Great Hunger*. London 1962

White, J. R. *Misfit*. London 1930

Wilkinson, Burke. *The Zeal of the Convert*. Buckinghamshire 1978

Winter, Sir Ormonde. *Winter's Tale*. London 1955

Wright, Arnold. *Disturbed Dublin*. London 1914

Wyndham, George. *Essays in Romantic Literature*. London 1919

Yeats, William Butler. *Autobiographies*. London 1955

Young, Ella. *Flowering Dusk*. New York 1945; *The Young Guard of Erin*. The Fianna Handbook.

Younger, Calton. *Ireland's Civil War*. London 1968; *A State of Disunion*. London 1972

Index

A. E. (George Russell), 22, 98, 99, 160
  and Irish co-operative movement 27–8, 143
  'The Inner and the Outer Ireland' 160
  'Open Letter' to Dublin employers (1913–) 57–8
Abbey Theatre, Dublin 73, 74, 100, 158
  foundation of 21–2
Abstentionist Parliament (Dail), *see* Dail
abstentionist policy 33–4, 113, 120
Achill Island 154
Aimes, Lieutenant Peter 165, 166
American (New York journal) 125
Amigo, Dr, Archbishop of Southwark 157
An Chlaidheamh Soluis (The Sword of Light) 48–9
An Ri (The King) (Pearse) 74
An tOglath ('The Young Warrior') 133n, 152
Anglo-Irish Treaty negotiations (1921) 154
Aran Islands 48
Ashe, Thomas 114–16, 157
Asquith, Herbert 39, 46, 47, 105
Auxies (Auxiliary police officers) 141–4, 150–1, 153, 160–1, 164, 168
Avory, Judge 107

Bachelor's Walk affair 61–2, 63
Bagalley, Captain 164, 166–7
Balbriggan, burning of 142
Balfour, Arthur 65
ballads, commemorating rebellion 100, 159
Ballinasloe, Tenants' Defence Association 11
Bannister, Gertrude 105
Barry, Kevin 158–9

Barry, General Tom 133, 135–6, 137–9, 142, 152, 153
Barton, Detective 127
Barton, Robert 122
Beaslai, Piaras 161
Belgian Congo, Casement's report on 35, 36–7
Bennett, Captain George 165, 166
Beresford, Lord 50
Berkeley, George 43
Bermingham, George 30, 38
Birkenhead, Lord 154
Black and Tans 141–4, 157–8, 160–1, 170–1
'Bloody Sunday' (November 21 1920) 165–72
Boer War 111
Boland, Harry 123, 154
Bonar Law, Andrew 44–5, 46, 171n
Boru, Brian 155
Brennan brothers 133
Brennan, Robert 161
Briolly, Silvain 124
British General Election (1918) 118
British League for Ulster 46
Broy, Eamonn 126, 128, 129, 153
Brugha, Cathal 92, 122, 165
Byrne, Vincent 190

Cairo Gang (group to crack IRA) 163–9
Campbell, Sir James, *see* Glenavy, Lord
Carrick-on-Shannon, burning of 142
Carson, Sir Edward 57, 107, 174
  and Ulster resistance to Home Rule 44–7, 49, 58, 60
Casement, Sir Roger 37–8, 102–12
  as arms buyer 60, 77, 79, 104
  as British diplomat 35, 36–7, 49, 102
  and Irish Volunteers 49, 58–9
  trial 105–12
Castlereagh, Lord 50

Ceannt, Eamonn 92, 93, 95
Cecil, Lord David 45
Chamberlain, Sir Austen 31
Chesterton, G. K. 69
  'The Napoleon of Notting Hill' 171
Childers, Erskine 60–1, 162
  The Riddle of the Sands 61
Childers, Molly 61
Churchill, Lord Randolph 44
Churchill, Sir Winston 31, 46, 64, 67,
  68
Citizen Army 54, 58, 77
Civil Disobedience 146–9; *see also*
  abstentionist policy; passive
  resistance
Clancy, Alderman George 164
Clancy, Peadar 166, 169–70
Clann na Gael (Irish-American
  Republican organization) 51, 75,
  79, 103, 146
  supplying weapons 71, 76–7
Clarke, Austin 78, 86
Clarke, Thomas 51, 52–3, 71, 93
Co-operative Movement 27–8, 143
Coffey, Dr. Dennis 69
Coholan, Judge 146
Colbert, Con 52–3, 95
Collins, Michael 122, 151–5, 171n,
  173
Collins, Michael,
  and 'Bloody Sunday' 163–7, 171–2
  and Easter Rising 91, 144
  re-organization of I.R.B. 114–15,
    124–32, 133n, 140
  understanding of finance 122–3,
    151–2
Collis, J. S. 159
Colum, Padraic 22, 27, 30, 98, 102
Conan Doyle, Sir Arthur 109–10
Connolly, James 25, 54–5, 71–2, 98,
  99
  and Easter Rising 77, 80–4, 87–8,
    91, 95–6
Connolly, John 83
Connolly, Sean 100
Conrad, Joseph 36
Conscription Bill for Ireland (1918)
  117, 163
Conservative Party, and Ulster
  Volunteers 45, 46–7, 107–9
Cooney, Andy 167
Cooper, Becky 170

Cork, activities of Auxiliaries in 142
Cork City, burning of 142–3
Cosgrave, W. T. 122, 155, 173–4
Costello, General Michael J. 9n
countryside, organization of
  Volunteer brigades in 133–40
Craig, James 46
Crawford, Colonel 60
Creagh, Lieutenant William 64
Croke Park shootings 170–1
Crooks, William 68
Cross, Colin, *The Fall of the British
  Empire* 13n
Crossbarry attack 138–9, 152
Crozier, General 164, 168
  Ireland Forever 47
Cuchulain 74
Cullen, Tom 128, 129, 130, 165
Curragh Mutiny (1914) 63–6, 163,
  176

Dail,
  declared illegal 124
  raising of loan 148–9, 151
  setting up of alternative
    government 120–3, 146–8
  since 1922 174–5
Daily Herald 162
Daily News 142
Daily Sketch 162
Dalton, Charlie 130, 131, 167
Dalton, Emmet 131–2
Daly, Edmund 82–3, 95
Daly, Paddy 128, 130, 131
Darling, Sir William 171n
Davitt, Michael 11, 49, 57, 76n
Davitt, Robert 49
de Valera, Eamon 38, 139
  American tour (1919) 145–6
  and Easter Rising 83, 92
  escape from jail 123
  personal charisma 113–14, 121–2,
    145–6
  and post-Treaty Ireland 173, 174
Deak, Francis 32, 33
Debbs, Eugene 55
Declaration of Rights 81–2
Devlin, Joe 170–1
Devoy, John 51, 75, 103–4, 146
Disraeli, Benjamin 16
'Ditch murder' (I.R.A. guerilla
  warfare) 135–9

Dockers Union 54
Dolan, Joe 128, 129, 131, 169
dual monarchy, Griffith's proposal of 34
Dublin,
 in 1900 23–8, 1920 150–1
 condition of working class 54
 general strike (1913) 54–8
Dunmanway, Co. Cork 134, 143
Dunraven, Lord 174
Dunsany, Lord 22
Dynamite Party, *see* Irish Republican Brotherhood

Easter Rising (1916) 79–97
 preparations for 71–2, 73–7
 reaction to 98–101, 113
Eluard, Paul 162
Emmet, Robert 97n, 145
Empire, British 11, 13–14
Esmonde, Sir Thomas 174
Evening News 169
evictions 12

Fenian Brotherhood 8, 9, 11, 76
 see also Clann na Gael
Fermoy, burning of 137
Fianna boys 84, 114
Fianna Fail party 174
Figgis, Darrell 102–3
 The Children of Earth 103
Fingall, Lady 23, 24–5, 69
First Born of the Coming Race (ideal of Irish literary renaissance) 22
Fischer, Louis 14
Fisk, Robert, *The Point of No Return* 176
Fitzalan, Lord 173
Fitzgerald, Captain 167
Fitzgerald, Desmond 161–2
Flanagan, Paddy 167
Flower, Robin 20
Fogarty, Dr, Bishop of Killaloe 164
French, Lord 87
Friends of Irish Freedom 146
Frongoch Internment Camp 113

GAA (Gaelic Athletic Association) 21, 51–2
Gaelic culture 20–2
 exclusion of in Garrison towns 134
Gaelic League 20–2, 27, 28, 102

and Irish Republican Brotherhood 51–2
 summer schools 37–8
Gandhi, Mahatma 14
Gandon, Richard 83
Garrison Irish 29
Garrison towns 134
Gavan Duffy, George 105, 106
Gay, Thomas 129
Geneva Convention 137
Germany 103–4, 110
 supply of weapons for Easter Rising 76–7, 78
Gibbon, Monk 96n
Gifford, Grace 94
Gladstone, W. E. 13, 15–16, 18–19, 33, 44
Glenavy, Lord (Sir James Campbell) 174
Gogarty, Oliver St John 90, 154–5
 and Griffith 30, 31, 32
 and Irish literary renaissance 22, 26–7
 as Senator 174
Goldsmith, Oliver 43
Gonne, Maud 25–6, 32, 34–5, 39, 95
Gore-Booth, Constance, *see* Markievicz, Countess
Gore-Booth, Sir Henry 26
Goose, Edmund 28
Gough, General Sir Hubert 63, 142
Granard, Earl of 174
Green, Alice Stopford 102
Greenwood, Sir Hamar 170
Gregory, Augusta, Lady 30, 118, 157–8
 and Irish literary renaissance 21–2, 25
 reaction to Easter Rising 98, 100
Grey, Sir Edward 67, 68
Griffin, Canon 143
Griffith, Arthur 29–35, 71, 164, 173
 abstentionist policy 33–4, 120–2
 establishment of Sinn Fein 32–5, 37
 passive resistance policy 30, 33–4, 113, 121, 149
 The Resurrection of Hungary 32
guerilla warfare 128, 135, 171
 Collins' development of 123, 125–7
 spread of from Ireland 137

Hague Convention 137
Haldane, Lord 118
Hammond, Colonel 87
Hardy, Lieutenant 166
Harris, Matthew 8–11, 76n
Hart, Christy 166
Hearst, William Randolph 110
Heuston, Sean 83, 95
Higginson, Brigadier-General 138
Hoey, Daniel 127
Home Rule 18, 39
    definition of 29
Home Rule Bill (1886) 13, 15, 44
Home Rule Bill (1912) 39–42, 66–7,
    103, 117, 162
Home Rule Party, *see* Irish
    Parliamentary Party
Horridge, Judge 107
Houlihan 129
Hudson, Colonel 137
Hungary, parallels with Irish
    situation 32, 33, 34, 37
hunger strikers 140, 156–7
Hyde, Douglas 20, 21

I.R.A.,
    Active Service Unit 150
    evolving from Irish Volunteers
        133n, 139
    recruitment to 133–6
    see also Irish Republican
        Brotherhood; Irish Volunteers
Igoe Gang 130, 150
Imperial Conference (1926) 174
Independent Newspaper Building 88
Inghini na hEireann (Daughters of
    Ireland) 26, 34–5
Ireland, Denis 18
Irish Agricultural Society 27
Irish Bulletin (Irish Government
    magazine) 161–2
Irish Catholic hierarchy 56–7, 117
Irish Convention (1917) 162
Irish Government Department of
    Publicity 161
Irish Independent (newspaper) 55–6,
    103
Irish Literary Theatre 73
Irish Parliamentary Party 16
    defeated by Sinn Fein 113–14,
        117–18, 120

and Home Rule Bill 39–40, 42, 49,
    117
and Parnell 18, 20
Irish Republican Army, *see* I.R.A.
Irish Republican Brotherhood
    (I.R.B.), distinct from IRA 133n
Irish Republican Brotherhood
    (I.R.B.) 50–3, 71, 103, 125, 128
    Intelligence Section 128–30
    Military Council 71, 73, 76–7, 79
    re-organised by Collins 114–15,
        124–32, 140
Irish Review (literary magazine) 72,
    102
Irish Socialist Republican Party 55
Irish soldiers
    and guerilla warfare 135–9
    in World War One 67–70, 100–1,
        117, 177
Irish Times 54, 147, 176
Irish Volunteers 66, 114
    arming of 60–2, 102–3
    and Citizen Army 58–9
    development into IRA 133n, 139
    and Easter Rising 79–92
    founding of 41, 48–50
    and I.R.B. 52–3, 71
    organisation in countryside 133–6
    see also Irish Republican
        Brotherhood
Irish Worker 71
Isaacs, Rufus, Lord Chief Justice 107

Jameson, Andrew 174
John, Augustus 28
Jones, Tom 171n
Joyce, James 18, 26–7, 31, 101, 130,
    164
    *A Portrait of the Artist as a Young
        Man* 19, 164
    Chamber Music 27
    Ulysses 170

Kavanagh, Sean 166, 169–70
Kee, Robert, *The Green Flag* 39
Kennedy, Rose 93
Kent, Edmund 83
Keogh, Tom 168
Kerr, Neil 129
Kettle, Professor Tom 29, 69, 101,
    117
King, Captain 166

King Lieutenant 169
Kitchener, Lord 69–70
Kossuth, Louis 37

labour strike, Dublin (1913) 54–8
Land Act (1903) 40n
Land League 11, 49
Larkin, Jim 54–8
Lavan, Martin 167–8
Lavery, Sir John, *The Funeral of Terence MacSwiney* 157
Lawrence, T. E. 103
Lawson, Sir Henry 134
Lenin 66
Leonard, Joe 130, 168
Lloyd George, David 31, 117, 162, 169, 171n, 173
Local Government Act (1898) 40n
Londonderry, Lord 45, 46
Lonergan, Michael 52–3
Long, Walter 124, 147
Lowe, Brigadier W. H. M. 87, 91–2
Lucas, Brigadier-General 137
Lynch, John 164, 166–7
Lynch, Liam 133, 136, 164
Lynch, Patrick 113

MacBride, John 32, 95, 99
McBride, Sean 150n
McCormack, John 130
MacDermott, Sean (Sean MacDiarmada) 71, 91, 93, 95
MacDonagh, Thomas 71, 72, 98–9
and Easter Rising 73–4, 77–8, 83–4, 92–3, 94
McFadden, Canon 102
McGilligan, Patrick 174
McGuinness, Joseph 113
McKee, Dick 165–6, 169–70, 172
MacKenna, Stephen 28, 86
McKeown, Sean 133
McLean, Lieutenant 167
McMahon 168
MacNamara 153–4
MacNeill, Eoin 41, 42, 48–50, 71, 79–80, 122
MacSwiney, Terence 156–8
Magner, Canon 143
Maguire, Sam 129
Mahaffy, Professor 80
Mallin, Michael 84, 92, 95
Mallow, burning of 142

Malone, Michael 92
Manchester Guardian 57, 110, 142, 162
Markievicz, Count Casimir 26
Markievicz, Countess (Constance Gore-Booth) 26, 57
in Dail 122
In Easter Rising 84–5, 92
and Sinn Fein 34–5, 38, 114
Martyn, Edward 21, 27, 73, 161
Maxwell, General Sir John 91
Mayo, Countess of 69
Mellows, Liam 52–3
Meredith, James Creed 146–7
Milligan, Alice 38
Milroy, Sean 123
Monteagle, Lord 147
Moore, Colonel Maurice 50
Moore, George 21, 22, 27, 28, 30, 50, 90
'A Drama in Muslin' 24
Morel, A. D. 36
Moreland, George (alias) 130–1
Morley, *Life of Gladstone* 16
Morris, William 21
Morrison, Major 171
Moylan, Sean 133
Mulcahy, Richard 114, 121, 122, 133n, 165
Murphy, William 55–6, 57
Murray, John 7

Nathan, Captain 164
National University, Dublin 40, 50
Nehru, Pandit 109
Neligan, Dave 128, 129
Newbury, Captain 167, 168
Nodnaya Volya (Russian Revolutionary group) 131
Northcliffe, Lord 160
Northern Ireland, *see* Ulster

O'Brien, Smith 12
O'Broin, Leon, *The Prime Informer* 65
O'Casey, Sean 22, 28, 53, 58, 89–90
The Lament for Thomas Ashe 115
O'Connell, Daniel 29, 34
O'Connell, Sean 166
O'Connolly, Sean 52–3
O'Connor, Sir James 47
A History of Ireland 47

O'Donnell, Frank Hugh 169
O'Donnell, Hugh, Earl of Tirconail 12
O'Duffy, Eoin 133
O'Faolain, Sean, *Bird Alone* 19
O'Farrell, Elizabeth 91
O'Flaherty, Liam 9
O'Hanrahan, Michael 95
O'Hegarty, P. S. 19, 51–2
O'Higgins, Kevin 174
O'Leary, John 52
O'Mara, James 146
O'Neill, Hugh, Earl of Tyrone 12
O'Rahilly 88–9, 91
O'Riann, Padraic 52–3
O'Shea, Katherine (Kitty) 17–18
O'Sullivan, Gearoid 169
O'Sullivan, Seamus 30, 31

Paget, Sir Arthur 63
Paris Peace Conference (1919) 121
Parliament Act (1911) 39
Parliament, British, reaction to Curragh mutiny 64–5
Parliamentary Party, *see* Irish Parliamentary Party
Parnell, Charles Stuart 16–9, 39, 65, 122, 155
    attitude to England 40
    political aims 11, 16–17, 29, 34
passive resistance policy 30, 33–4, 113, 121, 149
Pearse, James 74–5
Pearse, Padraic 49–50, 71–7, 98, 99
    and Easter Rising 79–82, 87, 88–9, 91–4
    support of Home Rule Bill (1912) 41–2)
Pearse, Willie 74, 93, 95
Pearson's Magazine 160
Percival, Major 137–8
physical force movement 11, 115, 121
    endorsement of 117
    see also Irish Republican Brotherhood (I.R.B.)
Plunkett, Count 113, 121, 122
Plunkett, Joseph 71, 72–4, 77, 82, 93–4
Plunkett, Sir Horace 27, 143, 147
Poe, Sir Hutchinson 174
poetry, inspired by Easter Rising 98–101

police,
    reprisals for IRA attacks 139–40
    see also Black and Tans
    structure of force 141–2
potato famine (1845–8) 12
Pound, Ezra 162
Proclamation of the Republic (1916) 81, 92–3, 121
Protestants,
    support of Gaelic League 20
    support for Irish independence 12, 22, 44n, 174
    in Ulster 43–4, 175–6

Redmond, Commissioner 127–8, 129
Redmond, John 49, 103, 113, 120, 177
    and Ireland in World War One 66–8, 71, 117
    support for Home Rule Bill (1912) 39–41, 75
Redmond, Major Willie 177
Redmond, William (John Redmond's son) 69
Renunciation Act (1782) 33
Republic of Ireland Act (1949) 175
Rice, Mary Spring 61
Richardson, Lieutenant-General 46
Risings against British rule,
    (1848) 8, 12
    (1867) 8
    see also Easter Rising
Roberts, Field-Marshal Lord 46, 64–5
Roche, Sergeant 131
Rooney, William 30
Rossa, O'Donovan 76
Russell, George, *see* A. E.
Russian Nihilism 156
Rutherford, Albert 167–8
Ryan, Ben 169–70
Ryan, Desmond 117

St. Enda's School, Rathfarnham 41–2, 74
Salisbury, Lord 64
Sargent, John Singer 28
'scorched earth' policy of Auxiliaries 142–3
separatism, Griffith's adaptation of 34
Shaw, George Bernard 28, 57

and Casement trial 106, 109–10
as Irish Protestant 44n
letter to *Daily News* on 1916
  executions 97n
Pygmalion 110
Sheehy, Mary 101
Shephard, Gordon 61
Sheridan 43
shoot to kill policy 176
Sinn Fein 115, 117
  election victories 34, 113–14, 118,
   120
  foundation of 32–3
  propaganda machine 161–2
  setting up of government 120–3,
   146–9, 161–2
  support for 39, 42, 147–9
Sinn Fein Arbitration and Land
  Courts 146
Sinn Fein District and Parish Courts
  147
Sinn Fein Supreme Court 147
Smith, Sir Frederick (F. E. Smith)
  46, 107–9, 112
Smyth, Colonel 139–40
Smyth, Detective 127
socialism, and Irish nationalism 28,
  55, 57–8, 71–2, 111
'Squad', the, (I.R.B. assassination
  group) 130–2, 168
Stack, Austin 146
Stalker, Assistant Chief Constable
  176
Stapleton, Bill 130, 131, 168, 170
Stead, Wickham 25
Stephens, James 28
  and Easter Rising 90, 98, 99–100
  and Griffith 30, 31, 38
  and Irish literary renaissance 22
  The Crock of Gold 28
  'Remembrance' 100
Stewart, Charles 16–19
Strickland, General 138
Sullivan, A. M. 40
Sullivan, Serjeant 105–9, 112
Sweetman, John 32
Swift, Jonathan 30–1, 43
Symonds, John Adington 22
Synge, John Millington 21–2, 25

Tagore, Rabindranath, *The Post
  Office* 74

Tain, The (story of Cuchulain) 74
Taylor, A. J. P. *English History
  1914–45* 118
Teeling, Frank 168
terror campaign by British,
  condemnation of 142
Thain, Private Ian 176
Thornton, Frank 128, 165
Times, The 124, 142, 160–1, 162
Tobin, Liam 128, 129, 130, 165, 169
Tobin, Richard 95–6
Transport Union 50, 54, 55
Treacy, Sean 131
Treaty (1922) establishing Irish
  independence 154, 173
Trim, burning of 142
Tuam, burning of 142
'Twelve Apostles, The' (IRB
  assassination group) 130–2
Tynan, Katherine 22, 95–6

Ulster,
  composition of 43
  failure of Northern Ireland
   Assembly 176
  resistance to Home Rule 43–7, 49,
   58, 60
  since 1922 175–7
Ulster Covenant (1912) 45–6
Ulster Provisional Government 46
Ulster Volunteers 44–7, 58, 69–70
  and Curragh Mutiny (1914) 60,
   63–4, 107–9
Ulster Workers' Council 176
Union, Act of (1800) 29, 33
Unionism, Griffith's appeal to 34
United Irishman (separatist
  newspaper) 30
United States,
  de Valera's visit to (1919) 145–6
  Fenians in 51, 145–6; *see also*
   Clann na Gael
  loan to Irish Republic 145, 146
  public opinion in 146, 160

Volunteers,
  in World War One 67–70, 100–1,
   117, 117
  see also I.R.A.; Irish Volunteers;
   Ulster Volunteers

Wallace, Henry 143
Wallace, William 106
White, George 167
White, Captain Jack, D.S.O. 58–9
Wilson, General Sir Henry 63–4,
  117, 158, 163
Wilson, Woodrow 109
Worker's Republic, The (newspaper)
  77
World War One,
  effect on Home Rule Bill 66–7
  Irish soldiers in 67–70, 100–1, 117,
  177
  as training ground for IRA 133,
  139

World War Two, Irish neutrality in
  174–5

Yeats, W. B. 27, 30, 157–8, 159–60
  and Irish literary renaissance 21–2,
    28, 74
  and Maud Gonne 25–6
  membership of I.R.B. 52
  as Senator 174
  letter to Lord Haldane (1918)
    118–20
  letter to *The Times* on terror
    campaign (1920) 160–1
  'Come Gather Round Me,
    Parnellites' 18–19
  'Easter 1916' 98–9